Neal-Schuman Library Technology Companion

NEAL-SCHUMAN
LIBRARY
TECHNOLOGY COMPANION

A BASIC GUIDE FOR LIBRARY STAFF

FOURTH EDITION

JOHN J. BURKE

An imprint of the American Library Association

Chicago // 2013

JOHN J. BURKE is the director of the Gardner-Harvey Library on the Middletown regional campus of Miami University (Ohio). He holds an MS in library science from the University of Tennessee and a BA in history from Michigan State University. John's past work experience includes service as both systems/public services librarian and program director for a web-based associate's degree in library technology at the University of Cincinnati–Raymond Walters College and also as a reference and electronic resources librarian at Fairmont State College (West Virginia). John is a past president of the Academic Library Association of Ohio (ALAO) and past chair of the Southwest Ohio Council on Higher Education (SOCHE) Library Council. He is the author of three previous editions of the *Neal-Schuman Library Technology Companion: A Basic Guide for Library Staff* (Neal-Schuman, 2001, 2006, and 2009), *IntroNet: A Beginner's Guide to Searching the Internet* (Neal-Schuman, 1999), and *Learning the Internet: A Workbook for Beginners* (Neal-Schuman, 1996). He has presented on a variety of technology topics at the Association of College and Research Libraries (ACRL) and American Library Association (ALA) conferences, the Library Information and Technology Association (LITA) National Forum, and various regional and state conferences. John may be reached at techcompanion@gmail.com.

Printed in the United States of America

17 16 15 14 13   5 4 3 2 1

Extensive effort has gone into ensuring the reliability of the information in this book; however, the publisher makes no warranty, express or implied, with respect to the material contained herein.

ISBNs: 978-1-55570-915-0 (paper); 978-1-55570-931-0 (PDF); 978-1-55570-932-7 (ePub); 978-1-55570-933-4 (Kindle).

Library of Congress Cataloging-in-Publication Data
Burke, John (John J.)
    Neal-Schuman library technology companion : a basic guide for library staff / John J. Burke. — Fourth edition.
      pages   cm
      Includes bibliographical references and index.
      ISBN 978-1-55570-915-0 (alk. paper)
      1. Libraries—Information technology. 2. Library science—Technological innovations. 3. Libraries and the Internet. I. Title. II. Title: Library technology companion.
    Z678.9.B85 2013
    025.00285—dc23   2013010846

Cover design by Kimberly Thornton. Images (c) Shutterstock, Inc.
Text design in Minion Pro and Gotham by Adrianna Sutton.

♾ This paper meets the requirements of ANSI/NISO Z39.48-1992 (Permanence of Paper).

CONTENTS

ILLUSTRATIONS

FIGURES

TABLES

PREFACE

Technology infuses every aspect of every day in every library, and thus basic technology skills are a prerequisite for everyone who works in a library. I designed the *Neal-Schuman Library Technology Companion: A Basic Guide for Library Staff*, Fourth Edition, to give colleagues a sound and sensible way to consider, access, and use library technologies to better meet the needs of our users. This book and its companion blog (http://techcompanion.blogspot .com) are designed to be a one-stop overview of all technologies used in libraries today.

The pages that follow describe the broad scope of systems, software, and specialized devices available to libraries and show how they are integrated into our institutions' unique processes. The book offers basic definitions, suggests applications and uses, considers adoption issues, and troubleshoots potential problems. All busy professionals need to learn how to evaluate these technologies and assess their usefulness, so the guide provides essential know-how in planning, security, purchasing, and more. Perhaps most important, a solid grounding in the topic will make library staff members more comfortable when speaking with colleagues or interacting with patrons.

This fourth edition of the guide revises the basics and explains the advances introduced in just the past few years. Web 2.0 technologies have become even more central to the work of library staff, social networks like Facebook and Twitter are used more heavily, open-source software is more established, and digital audio and streaming video continue to impact the way we all access and use media content. Chapter 1 is fully updated with the results of a second survey of technology skills and tasks among library staff members. Chapter 3 is fully updated with new sources for tracking down technology information. The chapters in the "Technology Tools for Libraries" section have all been revised to reflect new tools (like Pinterest and discovery layers) and new uses and aspects for the existing tools. The world of information technology changes at a relentless pace, and today's library managers, new librarians, support staff members, and students need a simple way to become informed and stay current.

The *Neal-Schuman Library Technology Companion* contains nineteen chapters arranged in five parts:

Part I, "Library Technology Basics," explores the basics.
>Chapter 1, "What Folks in the Trenches Know That You Should Too," provides context to the study of these information technologies and services by revealing the results of a second survey of working library staff members and the technologies they regularly use, and a comparison to the results of the survey in the third edition.
>Chapter 2, "The History of Information Technology in Libraries," delivers a historical overview of the technologies that have affected libraries.
>Chapter 3, "How to Find Information on Library Technologies," presents resources for learning more about the latest developments and issues.
>Chapter 4, "Evaluating, Buying, and Implementing Technology," offers a guide for appraising and purchasing equipment and putting systems into operation.

Part II, "Technology Tools for Libraries," examines the apparatus.
>Chapter 5, "Computers in Libraries: Desktops, Laptops, Mobile Devices, and Office Applications," shows how the computer has evolved and what its new uses allow, especially in terms of mobile devices.
>Chapter 6, "Computer Communication in Libraries: The Internet, Wi-Fi, and E-mail," takes on the wired and wireless world.
>Chapter 7, "Whither the Library Catalog? Library Systems, Discovery Layers, and Open-Source Options," reveals the vast changes and potential for the library catalog.
>Chapter 8, "Storage Devices in Libraries: Magnetic Media and Our Old Friend Paper," explains various techniques to record, retrieve, and access information.
>Chapter 9, "Library Databases and Electronic Resources: Full-Text Periodicals, E-books, and E-reference Collections," addresses this important and growing body of materials.

Chapter 10, "The Internet's Impact on Finding Information: *A* Is for Amazon, *G* Is for Google," explores both the technical and societal changes brought on by the Internet.

Chapter 11, "Web 2.0 and Libraries: Facebook, Twitter, YouTube, and Skype," marks the advent of new communication and social networking tools and technologies for interacting with our patrons.

Part III, "How Libraries Put Technology to Work," takes the information from the previous chapters and incorporates it into the day-to-day workflow.

Chapter 12, "Meeting and Supporting Patron Technology Needs: Universal Design and Adaptive/Assistive Technology," helps ensure that your technologies meet and serve the needs of your wide range of users.

Chapter 13, "Library 2.0 and the Library: Virtual Reference, Blogs, and Usability," emphasizes the importance of creating an Internet presence for your library with unique services for patrons.

Chapter 14, "How Library Staff Learn and Teach: Screencasts, Distance Learning, and Learning Management Systems," demonstrates how technology can aid in staff development and training.

Part IV, "Building and Maintaining the Technology Environment in Libraries," explores how to intelligently employ technology in everyday situations.

Chapter 15, "Protecting Technology and Technology Users: Spam, Spyware, and Security Strips," presents guidance for protecting the library and its patrons from the dangers of the cyberworld.

Chapter 16, "When Things Fall Apart: Troubleshooting Tips for Every Technology User," assesses typical problems and suggests ways to handle them as they arise.

Chapter 17, "Building the Technology Environment: Ergonomics, Infrastructure, and Gaming," will help make any facility comfortable and accessible.

Part V, "Where Library Technology Is Going and How to Get There," concludes the book.

Chapter 18, "Writing a Technology Plan," addresses the important issues of long-range planning and offers steps to start your planning process.

Chapter 19, "Our Technological Future: Ranganathan Meets Googlezon," looks ahead to how technology will continue to impact our tradition of service.

A glossary of useful terms is located at the end of the book. Terms found in the glossary appear in boldface within the text.

There is a great deal of information within these pages, but there is even more to discuss. Visit the companion blog at http://techcompanion.blogspot.com for updated resources and materials, as well as an opportunity to comment on the book. You may also reach the author with your questions and comments at techcompanion@gmail.com.

ACKNOWLEDGMENTS

I would like to thank my wife, Lynne, and children, Madeline, Anna, Philip, and Andrew; the many students and library staff members I have had the pleasure to teach through formal classes and workshops; and my colleagues at the Gardner-Harvey Library of Miami University Middletown for their guidance, help, and support in making this book possible.

I owe a great debt to the countless individuals who asked me technology questions, large and small, over the years. In the process of answering those questions I learned a lot about library technologies and what they are capable of (even when they do not work as advertised). I am grateful to ALA Editions and to my editor, Amy Knauer, for their encouragement and for this opportunity to pass my knowledge on to you.

Above all, I offer thanks to God for my family, my life, and the daily strength He gives me.

PART I
LIBRARY TECHNOLOGY BASICS

CHAPTER 1

WHAT FOLKS IN THE TRENCHES KNOW THAT YOU SHOULD TOO

AS LEWIS CARROLL WROTE in *Alice in Wonderland*, this book will "begin at the beginning." In this case, the beginning is to examine a premise that carries throughout this work: library technologies are ever-changing, and you need to have a working knowledge of them to succeed in library work. I rely on my own experience in libraries and my interactions with colleagues (as well as my attention to professional literature and electronic discussions) to help shape what I share in this book. I decided to also repeat the step I took in the third edition of the *Neal-Schuman Library Technology Companion*: what if I asked library staff members from all types of libraries to tell me what technologies and technology skills they use regularly? The remainder of this chapter describes the survey from this edition, how it compared to the survey from the third edition, and what I learned from it.

LIBRARY TECHNOLOGY SKILLS SURVEY

In the spring of 2012, I offered a second version of the survey I originally used in the fall of 2008. The hope, as before, was to gain insight into the regular technology tasks of library staff members. The survey consisted of eight questions (nine in 2008). It was posted to a variety of electronic discussion groups focused on academic libraries, public libraries, library technology experts, library support staff members, school librarians, special librarians, and catalogers (see Table 1.1). The survey was designed to be available for three weeks, and I hoped to gain at least as many responses as I did in 2008 (1,800) from a diverse group of individuals working in libraries. That earlier total was a complete surprise, as I had only hoped for around 200 responses. In the end, my hopes were once again exceeded by receiving 2,075 responses. This was a wonderful sample to work with in assessing **technology** use.

Table 1.1

Library electronic discussion groups where the survey was posted

Discussion Group Mailing List Address	Affiliated Institution
academic_division@sla.lyris.net	Special Libraries Association (SLA) Academic Division
alao@lists.uakron.edu	Academic Library Association of Ohio (ALAO)
autocat@listserv.syr.edu	Library Cataloging and Authorities Discussion Group (Syracuse University)
cjc-l@ala.org	Association of College and Research Libraries (ACRL) Community and Junior Colleges Section (CJCLS)
collib-l@ala.org	ACRL College Libraries Section (CLS)
ili-l@ala.org	ACRL Information Literacy Instruction Section
infolit@ala.org	American Library Association (ALA) Information Literacy Discussion List
libsup-l@u.washington.edu	Library Support Staff (University of Washington)
lis-infoliteracy@jiscmail.ac.uk	Chartered Institute of Library and Information Professionals (CILIP) Information Literacy Group
lis-pub-libs@jiscmail.ac.uk	UK Public Libraries
lita-l@ala.org	Library and Information Technology Association (LITA)
lm_net@listserv.syr.edu	School Library Media and Network Communications (Syracuse University)
oclsconf@ls2.cmich.edu	Attendees of and presenters at the Off-Campus Library Services biennial conference
offcamp@listserv.utk.edu	Off-Campus Library Services Section (University of Tennessee, Knoxville)

Table 1.1 (continued)

Discussion Group Mailing List Address	Affiliated Institution
ohiolink@lists.ohiolink.edu	OhioLINK Consortium
oplinlist@oplin.org	Ohio Public Libraries
publib@webjunction.org	OCLC Public Librarianship
sla-ccin@sla.lyris.net	Special Libraries Association– Cincinnati Chapter
sla-ccle@sla.lyris.net	Special Libraries Association– Cleveland Chapter
sla-ccno@sla.lyris.net	Special Libraries Association– Columbus Chapter
sla-dite@sla.lyris.net	Special Libraries Association– IT Division
tslibrarians@listserv.kent.edu	Technical Services Librarians and Catalogers (Kent State University)
univers@infoserv.inist.fr	International Federation of Library Associations and Institutions (IFLA) Academic and Research Libraries Section
web4lib@listserv.nd.edu	Web Technologies in Libraries (University of Notre Dame)

DEMOGRAPHICS OF THE RESPONDENTS

Despite the large response and the diversity of electronic discussion groups selected, the respondents are not a perfect cross-section of library staff from all types of libraries: 64 percent work in academic libraries, 20 percent in public libraries, 9 percent in school libraries, and 7 percent in special libraries. In terms of their education, they were also not a broad-based sample: just under 80 percent listed a master's of library science (MLS) degree, other master's degree, or other graduate work as their highest level of education. In the 2012 survey I asked respondents to choose from a list all of the task areas that they perform at their libraries, rather than just choosing a single primary

Table 1.2 Job tasks performed on a regular basis

Task	Number of Selections	Percentage of Respondents
Reference	1,358	66.0
Instruction	1,290	62.7
Collection development	1,180	57.3
Circulation	784	38.1
Cataloging	776	37.7
Library/IT systems	731	35.5
Marketing/public relations	702	34.1
Library administration	695	33.8
Outreach	684	33.2
Acquisitions	639	31.0
Periodicals/serials	571	27.7
Media/audiovisuals	550	26.7
Distance library services	462	22.4
Interlibrary loan	453	22.0
Archives/special collections	297	14.4
Other	262	12.7

area of responsibility. Table 1.2 shows a distribution of tasks among respondents, but certainly a number of public services–related tasks fall at the upper end.

Most of the "Other" choices were somewhat more specific aspects of the choices listed on the survey (e.g., "website," "staff selection," "user experience"). Finally, in terms of their careers in libraries, 19 percent have worked for five or fewer years, 20 percent between six and ten years, 30 percent between eleven and twenty years, and 31 percent for twenty-one or more years.

THE MOST COMMON TECHNOLOGIES AND SKILLS

Despite the demographic mismatches to the larger population of library staff members, I still believe that the respondents' answers provide a clearer vision

Table 1.3   Technologies and skills used on a regular basis, chosen by more than 50 percent of respondents

Technology or Skill	Number of Selections	Percentage of Respondents
E-mail	2,015	97.6
Word processing	1,943	94.1
Using a web browser	1,931	93.6
Web searching	1,931	93.6
Searching library databases	1,894	91.8
Spreadsheets (Microsoft Excel, etc.)	1,760	85.3
Library catalog (public side)	1,742	84.4
Public or staff printers	1,653	80.1
Teaching others to use technology	1,651	80.0
Presentation software (Microsoft PowerPoint, Prezi, etc.)	1,551	75.1
Scanners and similar devices	1,401	67.9
Troubleshooting technology	1,355	65.6
Library management system (staff side)	1,248	60.5
File management/operating system navigation skills	1,239	60.0
Creating online instructional materials/products (LibGuides, tutorials, etc.)	1,236	59.9
Educational copyright knowledge	1,130	54.7
Fax machine	1,035	50.1

of the universe of technology skills used in libraries. Respondents were asked to select from a list the technologies or technology skills that they used on a regular basis in their jobs. Table 1.3 shows the seventeen items from the list that were chosen by more than 50 percent of respondents.

It is interesting to see that the top five skills from the list have essentially remained the same as they were in the 2008 survey (using a web browser snuck up the list a bit). These are clearly essential skills for more than 90 percent of respondents: e-mail, word processing, using a web browser, web searching, and searching library **databases**. The next four skills are still required of 80 percent or more respondents: spreadsheets, the public library catalog, printers, and teaching others to use technology (printers moved into this category since 2008). This group of eight shows what most library staff members should have in their skill sets to meet job requirements in various settings. The list is a good guide to skills the majority of library staff should aspire toward mastering.

The skills showing the biggest increases from 2008 to 2012 include creating online instructional materials/products (16.9 points higher), instant messaging (15.5 points higher), presentation software (15 points higher), scanners and similar devices (10.1 points higher), educational copyright knowledge (7.1 points higher), and spreadsheets (7 points higher).

As we move further down the list, there is a great diversity of skills still expected of a large percentage of the respondents. Table 1.4 shows skills that were chosen by less than 50 percent of the respondents. Some were not as common as I expected (e.g., tweeting) while others are more prominent than I thought they might be (e.g., educational copyright knowledge). I was heartened to see a strong representation of people who "make technology purchase decisions" as that capacity should be on hand at various levels of the organization. The rarest skills appeared to be those connected to more specialized information technology (IT) activities, which perhaps is not a surprise. On a lighter note, I was rooting for Google Docs, which is now Google Drive, to overtake fax machines (because I use Google Drive frequently and we no longer have a dedicated fax machine in our library—though we do fax through the web), but my hopes did not prevail.

THE MOST COMMON WISHES FOR
TECHNOLOGIES AND SELF-DEVELOPMENT

I also asked respondents to answer two additional questions: (1) What technology skill could you learn to help you do your job better? and (2) What

Table 1.4 Technologies and skills used on a regular basis, chosen by less than 50 percent of respondents

Technology or Skill	Number of Selections	Percentage of Respondents
Google Docs	1,020	49.4
Instant messaging, chatting, or texting	992	48.1
Designing or managing a library website	923	44.7
Creating webpages	905	43.8
Database software (Microsoft Access, etc.)	826	40.0
Facebook	823	39.9
Making technology purchase decisions	794	38.5
Installing software	786	38.1
Using a learning management system (LMS) or virtual learning environment (VLE)	778	37.7
Blogging	624	30.2
Computer security knowledge	559	27.1
Graphic design	471	22.8
Installing technology equipment	461	22.3
Tweeting (Twitter)	429	20.8
Assistive/adaptive technology	365	17.7
Computer programming or coding	262	12.7
Network management	207	10.0
Other	197	9.5

technology or technology skill would you most like to see added to your library? Answers to the first question were all over the map, with one respondent stating, "Technology is always changing, always learning." *Better, advanced,* and *more* were repeatedly applied as adjectives for skills with a number of technologies. High on several people's future training agendas were programming or coding, web design, and network management. One respondent said, "I'd like a feeling for the big picture and how all of the parts go together."

Nearly 700 respondents did not suggest any additional technology skills to learn; another 100 replied that they did not have a need for additional technology skills. Most of the latter group gave no additional comment or explanation, though some shared that their jobs did not require them (or would not allow them) to use more technology, and others held that technology is not the answer to all library-related problems—no argument here. One person captured the difficulty of fitting professional development into a busy schedule: "Anything. We have no IT person. As the Director, I am learning more about computers and how they work on a daily basis. Most of what I learn is by doing a Google search/trial and error." Another noted, "I need to be more comfortable with the equipment we loan to patrons—cameras, iPads, etc."

On adding technologies to their libraries or technology skills for themselves or their coworkers, respondents' replies ran the gamut. *Mobile* and *social* were repeated adjectives, and Facebook, RFID, iPads, computers, and LibGuides were popular technology choices. Discovery layers and new library systems were mentioned. Talents in web design, Web 2.0 technologies, programming, and graphic design were strongly sought. Rather than adding new technologies or talents, there were also calls for more staff on hand to deal with current technologies ("A Digital Librarian and ITS group that caters to nontech staff") and for greater comfort and abilities from current staff. As one respondent put it, "I wish all staff could do basic troubleshooting." On the more positive side, another respondent seemed confident that his or her library will keep up: "It will be whatever is developed next. I feel our building is forward thinking."

WHAT CAN WE LEARN FROM THE SURVEY

Clearly every library position and every library setting is different. Without a doubt, the survey could have been more representative. My hope is that the results give you, as they have given me, a confirmation that we all need to grow our abilities in this common palette of skills. As well, there are many other tasks and capacities (both on the survey and suggested by the respondents) that may well become expected of us as new technologies arrive and our libraries change. The chapters ahead will help you become more aware and develop your knowledge. My recommendation is to turn the page and "go on till you come to the end: then stop."

QUESTIONS FOR REVIEW

1. What are the top ten technologies or technology skills required in your position?
2. Were you surprised by anything in the survey results?
3. What technology skill could you learn to help you do your job better?
4. What technology or technology skill would you most like to see added to your library or your library staff?
5. Who is responsible for providing training in new resources and services in your library?

Selected Sources for Further Information

Crawford, Walt. 2008. "Making It Work Perspective: TechNos and TechMusts." *Cites and Insights* 8, no. 4. http://citesandinsights.info/v8i4d.htm.

Walt examines various lists (his own and those of other bloggers) of technology skills that individual "techie" librarians lack and those that are recommended for every library staff member to have. He examines the interplay of which technology abilities are accepted as needed for all staff and suggests that absolutism is not the best expectation.

Ennis, Lisa A. 2008. "Talking the Talk: Communicating with IT." *Computers in Libraries* 28, no. 8: 14–17.

Ennis provides a short list of tips for getting along with the IT professionals in your environment.

Gutsche, Betha, ed. 2012. *Competency Index for the Library Field.* Dublin, OH: OCLC WebJunction. www.webjunction.org/documents/webjunction/Competency_Index_for_the_Library_Field.html.

The webpage links to a document of definitions for various tasks arranged by competency area for all work in libraries, with sections that focus on core technology skills—very useful for identifying expectations for various staff positions.

Thompson, Susan M., ed. 2009. *Core Technology Competencies for Librarians and Library Staff: A LITA Guide.* New York: Neal-Schuman.

This group of essays addresses in more detail the expectations for a variety of library positions in public and academic libraries. It also addresses ways in which to measure and develop these technology competencies.

Walter, Scott, and Karen Williams, eds. 2010. *The Expert Library: Staffing, Sustaining, and Advancing the Academic Library in the 21st Century.* Chicago: Association of College and Research Libraries.

This collection of essays assesses what competencies are needed as libraries change while incorporating new technologies and services. Specific advice is given to aid the job redefinition and hiring process.

CHAPTER 2

THE HISTORY OF INFORMATION TECHNOLOGY IN LIBRARIES

LIBRARIES HAVE LONG played an essential role in containing, preserving, and sharing information. Countless civilizations have, over thousands of years, produced and relied on various types of information, from creation stories to herd counts to tax rolls. These facts, philosophies, and communications were recorded because individuals in these societies saw some purpose in sharing such lore and information with others in the present and in preserving it for future generations. The explosion of information we have seen over the past three decades is merely the latest skirmish in a long-running battle: How can societies maintain their collections of facts, history, images, data, and fiction as the amount of these items increases so rapidly? Over thousands of years, libraries were adopted as a mechanism for accomplishing these purposes; were it not for libraries, we would have little or no knowledge of past generations or civilizations.

At each step along the way, libraries would have failed in their efforts without **information technology** (**IT**). We tend to imagine technology as specifically involving computers and electronic devices, but technology encompasses both the products and processes that people create. Handling information requires a diverse collection of practical tools and processes. Looking at technology in the library world, processes would include the methods for rebinding books or classifying the items in a collection, and full-text periodical databases or mobile devices are examples of products. Information technology as a whole, then, includes any items or methods for containing, transmitting, and storing information.

TRENDS IN LIBRARY TECHNOLOGIES

Two main goals have driven library use of technology: better serving the needs of the library's community and streamlining the workflow of the staff.

The technologies that have impacted and continue to impact the library world fall into three main groups: (1) those created specifically for libraries and library work, (2) those created within the larger world and adapted for use in libraries, and (3) those created in the world and brought into libraries without much alteration.

The first group would encompass developments such as Melvil Dewey's classification system, the card catalog, and the **machine-readable cataloging** (**MARC**) record. In the second group we find such examples as the creation of library management systems that enable online catalogs and manage circulation and cataloging, the continuing molding of Internet-based databases by vendors to fit library needs, and libraries' own alterations of website design for internal purposes. We see many examples of the third group in staff use of standard technology, such as e-mail, telephones, copiers, bar-code readers, and many computer applications.

TEN KEY DEVELOPMENTS IN INFORMATION TECHNOLOGY

Many information technologies have been created over the years. The library itself is a technology developed to handle information storage and retrieval. This section discusses ten key historic developments in information technology that have affected libraries and their work over the centuries, in roughly chronological order. Some of these technologies are still in full use today, whereas others have been replaced or had their roles reduced. They represent processes for retaining or organizing information as well as manufactured tools or other products. All technology is designed to meet a particular need, and while few needs ever disappear completely, humanity is always finding new ways to better address long-standing needs. It is important to remember the former roles of obsolete technologies as we look at today's technologies and toward the technologies that may replace them in the future.

Development 1: Writing and Paper

The development of written language and alphabets is the starting place for a discussion of information gathering. Writing's roots can be seen in prehistoric cave paintings—an early pictographic method of communicating information by drawing symbols and pictures to represent concepts. Pictographs allow individuals to preserve information (at least in the short term) for their own use and also to share with others. If one writes on something that will last (the next key development in technology for libraries), the information can be passed on beyond the life of that individual and perhaps for many generations.

Compare writing to another method for passing information along through time: memorization. In many cultures, skilled individuals (e.g., *griots* in West Africa) were able to memorize genealogies, stories, and historic cultural events and recount them as needed. Each oral traditionalist or story-teller would train someone, usually beginning in childhood, to memorize the information and pass it on to succeeding generations. While memorization can be an effective way to preserve sets of information, there are some dif-ficulties for its long-term use.

First, because only one person or a small number of people can remem-ber the information, there is the danger of accidents, contagions, or untimely deaths completely wiping out the information. In addition, access to the information is limited because only those who have memorized it can reveal it. Second, because the information is memorized in a distinct pattern, it can be difficult for the accountable person to recall individual bits of informa-tion (e.g., the date of a battle, the name of an individual's daughter) without recounting larger parts of what he or she has memorized. Third, even with exceptional effort at memorization, some details are bound to be lost or cor-rupted. Intentional corruption can also easily occur because there is no writ-ten record to use for comparison. The safety of, access to, and integrity of the memorized information are major problems, which a written record can overcome.

The physical item that an individual is writing on has a huge impact on how easy it is to pass the information along. There are two elements of pass-ing information to consider: time and distance. Cave paintings are handy to show to folks who live nearby and to share with future generations, but they are awfully difficult to send to a friend in the next valley. This element of transporting information guided the development of writing material from cave walls, to stone tablets, to papyrus scrolls, to goatskin or calfskin (vellum), to linen- and now tree-based paper. Paper is relatively cheap to produce in quantity, is lightweight, and can last for a fairly long period of time.

Development 2: The Printing Press and Books

With a system of writing and a medium to place it on, the communication of ideas could be accomplished relatively easily and cheaply. Paper writings were bound into books (as vellum had been) and passed along. However, making multiple copies of a work remained a laborious process.

Enter the Gutenberg revolution of the fifteenth century. The invention of movable type and the printing press first in China, and then independently in Europe by Gutenberg, gave people the ability to make their writings available to a larger audience at a much quicker pace. Humanity entered into a time period in which improvements and innovations changed the publishing process and the audience for books. Printing became faster, paper grew cheaper, and literacy increased among the populace. These changes set the stage for libraries to develop on a large scale: many books were being printed and people wanted to read them. Libraries had existed in earlier civilizations (notably among the Babylonians, Romans, and Greeks) but had been available to only a small elite. Printing allowed information to reach a wider audience and libraries to serve as intermediaries between the growing amounts of literature and a growing literate population.

Development 3: Classification Systems

Libraries have had to deal with ever-increasing amounts of printed materials since the dawn of the printing press. Once the number of books in a library exceeded the librarian's memory, a method for locating a specific item or finding materials on a topic was needed. One major breakthrough in organizing and using this information was the development of **classification systems**.

Unlike today, where libraries tend to choose among two or three "universal" systems, classification schemes of the past were tied to a given library or collection, meeting the local needs of that particular entity. Every library featured its own way to organize materials by broad categories of knowledge. A tremendous change came about in 1876 with the development of the Dewey Decimal System. Melvil Dewey's subject-oriented system for organizing books caught on and was adopted by a large number of libraries. Today, 95 percent of public and school libraries and 25 percent of academic libraries use the system. The Library of Congress Classification System, developed to organize that library's immense holdings, was later adopted by libraries (primarily academic ones) as an alternative standard. Both systems work on a similar principle: arrangement of the collection by the subject matter of the item.

Classification systems helped libraries tame the growing mass of information. With them, library users could freely browse the collection by topic to find what they needed. The adoption of standardized systems also let libraries work together more smoothly and made it easier for patrons to understand how to use multiple libraries. With this innovation in place, libraries could move to make their service more efficient and their users' experiences more fruitful.

Development 4: The Card Catalog

The creation and standardization of a tool to help people locate the information in a library was an impressive development in information technology. While libraries had been organized by local models of classification system for years, the invention of the **card catalog** in 1791 in France (using the backs of playing cards, which at the time were blank), and the substantial growth of its use by libraries from the 1850s onward, gave library users an additional method for finding items beyond browsing the shelves. It also enhanced the work of libraries in at least two ways. First, it improved the ability of the library staff to locate materials and therefore provide service to their patrons. The card catalog allowed the library's collection to be searched from one location without having to browse and scan the shelves. It added convenience as well as the ability to use multiple entry points (author, title, and subject) to access the collection.

Second, the creation of a relatively easy-to-use tool to find library information allowed the public to participate directly in the research process. The catalog was fairly straightforward: if you wanted to find books by Louisa May Alcott, you looked in the drawers for the As and then browsed through the cards until you found her works. Once catalogs became standardized, it was easy for patrons to walk into any library and see what was available on a subject, written by a given author, or confirm whether a given title was held. The card catalog was the first example of an end-user searching tool: the patron gained the freedom to search, and library staff discovered a new instructional endeavor.

Development 5: Library Systems and the MARC Record

With classification systems and card catalogs in use, libraries were doing a fine job of managing information. There came a point, however, when individuals in the profession saw there could be easier ways to manage large collections of materials and provide access to the catalog for a large number of users. They looked to the power of computers to help make libraries more efficient. Several libraries joined forces with computing professionals in the late 1960s to create the first **automated** library systems and their descendants, which operated from large mainframe computers and had "dumb" terminals for library staff and users to access the systems. Each item in the catalog was represented in a MARC record, which contains bibliographic information along with subject headings, call numbers, and other useful information (see Figures 2.1 and 2.2 for current examples). As we will see in Chapter 7, these systems allow libraries to keep track of the items they own and are circulating

Figure 2.1   Screenshot of an OPAC record for an item

without a large number of cards and paper. The quest for these systems drove libraries into the computer age, setting the foundation for the today's world of digital information.

Development 6: Personal Computers

Personal computers (PCs) have made a huge impact on society, including in libraries (see Chapter 5). PCs increased libraries' computing power and allowed greater flexibility in choosing their local office and **management software** than was possible with mainframes. PCs also provided a platform for libraries to experiment with new media types, such as CD-ROMs (compact disc read-only memory), and to start accessing **remote information services** (periodical and shared cataloging databases, and eventually the Internet). In a relatively short period of time, libraries moved from having just one or two PCs in the back room to offering dozens of machines to the public. Today's library is unimaginable without the personal computer as both a staff resource and as a means for the public to access library resources.

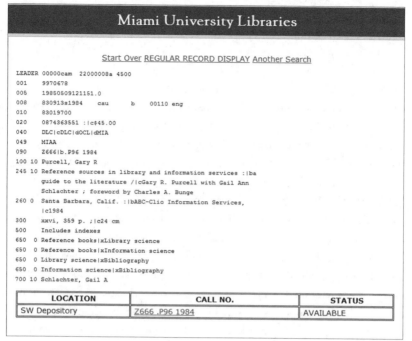

Figure 2.2   Screenshot of a MARC record for the same item

Development 7: Online Searching

An exciting development of the computer age for libraries was the ability of companies to start computerizing periodical indexes and other resources and then provide them to libraries using a telephone line and a modem. Starting in the 1970s, libraries were able to access resources they could not afford to keep in house and to search these electronic resources much more easily than could be accomplished by manually paging through their print predecessors. Companies such as Dialog, BRS, and LexisNexis offered libraries access to periodical indexes and full-text newspapers, magazines, journals, and reference sources. Users would choose one or more indexes or periodicals to search and then enter terms to locate related citations, **abstracts**, or articles.

For the first time, libraries had to contend with having resources available that they did not physically own as the advent of **online searching** occurred. Connecting to these online services could be expensive (users were charged a set fee per minute), but many libraries were willing to offer this service to their patrons. Early online searching was done by library staff members, partly because the command language for searching was difficult to learn and partly because of the expensive connection fees. Eventually, the methods of searching grew easier (and pricing plans began to change) and library patrons, known as end users, could more successfully attempt searching on their own. The move toward our current situation of the virtual, online library was under way.

Development 8: Audiovisual or Media Items

As with computers, audiovisual or **media items** were created within society at large and came to libraries as a new way of packaging information. Adding media items such as **videocassettes**, compact discs, and DVDs to libraries over the years (see Table 2.1) changed the complexion of the collection. These new media also caused challenges for the staff in terms of their shelving, location, and protection. In the past, libraries may have had only the book version of a popular title; today, a library is likely to need to find space for the book and various versions of the book in media formats. For example, consider J. K. Rowling's *Harry Potter and the Deathly Hallows*: A library might have the book, compact disc (abridged or unabridged) audiobook versions of the book, DVDs of the two movies made from the book, and compact discs of the two movie soundtracks. In addition, the same library may also have digital versions of any of these (e.g., videos, downloadable .mp3s from the soundtrack, e-books). The rich diversity of nonbook formats has allowed libraries to better serve today's communities, who expect to have access to a wide variety of media. The consumers' expectations that these kinds of media will be included in collections caused libraries to rethink their collection development and organization practices and to more readily adopt new media. *Audiovisuals* is the more historic term, but it is still used in some libraries. *Media* has become a fairly common replacement term, with some collection areas in libraries labeled only with the type of item included in them (e.g., DVDs).

Development 9: The Internet

The Internet has had a strong presence in libraries and library planning for nearly twenty years. From the early days of library **Gopher sites** and the first websites to today's full-text periodical indexes, e-books, and virtual reference, the Internet has become a mainstay of the library world. The Internet continues to stimulate library staff to retool their delivery of services to patrons and to reconsider how they can best present the wealth of free online information alongside library-purchased print and digital resources. Libraries now use the Internet as a delivery mechanism to access resources and provide them to patrons within and without the library. They offer to help library patrons by answering reference questions via text messaging, instant

Table 2.1 Timeline of invention dates for audiovisual items

Audiovisual Medium	Date Invented
Phonograph LP record	1948
Audiocassette	late 1950s
VHS videocassette	1976
Videodisc	1978
Compact disc	1982
CD-ROM	1984
MP3	1993
DVD	late 1990s
iPod	2001
iPhone	2007
Amazon Kindle	2007
iPad	2010

Note: The dates for CD-ROMs and earlier media were taken from Walt Crawford's *Current Technologies in the Library: An Informal Overview* (Boston: G. K. Hall, 1988).

messaging (IM), e-mail, or chat in an attempt to assist no matter the time of day or where patrons are located. They are working to organize websites and library-licensed resources to help patrons find what they need. Libraries can claim many Internet successes yet still face several challenges from this work in progress. In a world of ever-present access to information, where does the library fit in? This topic is discussed in subsequent chapters.

Development 10: A Techno-Savvy Populace and a Society That Requires Technology

Developments in libraries are, and should be, driven in part by the expressed needs and expectations of each library's community. As noted, with some of the earlier developments on this list, society often created something new and libraries decided to include it in their collections. This process has been influenced and driven by our patrons requesting items or by people in our communities taking an interest in new media or services before we actually adopt them. Look for the receptiveness of our communities to new technologies to continue to shape libraries in the future.

Technology demands are not always driven by user choice, however. As society grows more dependent on various information technologies, some patrons find themselves caught in the digital divide. They are often required to use computers or access materials on the Internet to complete homework or fill out government forms or pursue commercial activities, and yet some patrons cannot afford access to the required technologies. Libraries are taking on the responsibility of providing this access.

WHAT ARE LIBRARIES USING TODAY?

We find libraries today using a wide variety of technologies. Most have online catalogs and offer public **Internet access** through desktop computers and Wi-Fi (wireless Internet access). Most include a number of different formats for storing information: books, periodicals, electronic reference sources, DVDs, streaming media, and e-books. Libraries as a whole are spending increasing amounts of money on electronic resources and the infrastructure to support them, often at the expense of traditional, print-based materials. Further, the more libraries invest in electronic resources, the less flexible they can be in choosing whether to continue with these expenditures. With this impact in mind, it is crucial for us to understand library technologies to help make the right decisions for our libraries and our patrons. The rest of this book looks at current library technologies in detail and examines what the future may hold.

QUESTIONS FOR REVIEW

1. What are the three groups into which library technologies could be placed?
2. What current technology, in your view, could have as large an impact as the ten key developments in this chapter?
3. Is there an unmentioned key development that you would add into the list of ten?
4. How would you define the term *technology*?
5. Describe the impact that you have seen one of the ten developments have in your own library.

Selected Sources for Further Information

Aqili, Seyed Vahid, and Alireza Isfandyari Moghaddam. 2008. "Bridging the Digital Divide: The Role of Librarians and Information Professionals in the Third Millennium." *Electronic Library* 26, no. 2: 226–237.

This article provides an overview of the digital divide and the roles that librarians and information professionals can play in bridging it.

Battles, Matthew. 2004. *Library: An Unquiet History*. New York: W. W. Norton.

Battles's book is an intriguing look at the ancient origins of libraries and their development into the modern age.

Crawford, Walt. 1988. *Current Technologies in the Library: An Informal Overview*. Boston: G. K. Hall.

This source gives an excellent history of the technologies available in 1988, from microfilm to computers.

Lerner, Frederick A. 1998. *The Story of Libraries: From the Invention of Writing to the Computer Age*. New York: Continuum.

This book provides an excellent history of libraries and librarianship.

Lester, June, and Wallace C. Koehler Jr. 2007. *Fundamentals of Information Studies: Understanding Information and Its Environment*. 2nd ed. New York: Neal-Schuman.

The book includes an overview of library and information science with references to historic developments in the field.

Musmann, Klaus. 1993. *Technological Innovations in Libraries, 1860–1960: An Anecdotal History*. Westport, CT: Greenwood Press.

This is an interesting history of library technologies developed, adopted, or adapted during a century of monumental change for libraries.

Sharma, Ravindra N., ed. 2012. *Libraries in the Early 21st Century: An International Perspective*. Vol. 1. Berlin: Walter de Gruyter.

This collection provides individually authored chapters on the history and development of libraries worldwide with a special focus on technology.

Wiegand, Wayne A. 1996. *Irrepressible Reformer: A Biography of Melvil Dewey*. Chicago: American Library Association.

Wiegand's work provides a full history of Dewey's life and his impact on librarianship, from his invention of the classification system to his work in the American Library Association (ALA) and his efforts to professionalize library work.

CHAPTER 3

HOW TO FIND INFORMATION ON LIBRARY TECHNOLOGIES

BECAUSE TECHNOLOGY EVOLVES at a rapid pace, it is never enough to simply know about and understand the technology owned by a single library. You need to know where you can learn more about technology, whether you are responsible for planning for new technology or trying to understand and use what is already in your library (and what is yet to come). This chapter discusses some places to turn to find answers to technology questions. Knowing where to look for technology facts can be very empowering; it can give you the confidence that you can find an answer. As with library reference work, it is more important—and more feasible—to know where to look for technology information rather than to know all the information yourself.

REASONS TO USE TECHNOLOGY INFORMATION SOURCES

There are many reasons in library work to search for information on technologies—both general and library-specific ones. Following are the four most common reasons people who work in libraries search for information on technology:

> *For general awareness.* As noted, technology is changing rapidly and we need to keep up with current trends. A library organization can feel overwhelmed by the plethora of new choices on the market and new desires on the part of staff or the community. Library personnel need some sense of what is on the cutting edge and how it may apply to libraries. My views on the future of technologies in libraries continue to change based on the information I find and the trends I discover. You may not wish to follow every new development in technology,

but you will benefit from using a reliable source of information to keep you abreast of major happenings.

To compare products and services. As libraries try to find technology solutions to fulfill the service needs of their communities, they often need to compare a number of similar products. This occurs when a library is searching for a specific product or service to meet its needs or when a competitive bidding process is required for purchasing technology. Turning to the opinions of library colleagues, comparisons in journals, or other sources of advice and information can be very helpful. Suggestions of specific technologies or solutions can then be sought out and compared to determine the best option.

To find a known product or service. When specific product or service solutions are already identified, a library will need to locate information about them. The information might be descriptions provided by a vendor, critical reviews in formal publications, or the advice and experiences of colleagues. Some things that a library may want to find out include (1) where a product can be purchased, (2) specific pricing information, (3) the success or failure in use of the item in libraries, and (4) suggestions for, and comparisons with, alternative products.

To configure existing technology. Once a technology is in place in a library, the questions do not end. Libraries always need more information about installing a product, configuring it to work correctly with other products, and troubleshooting problem situations. At times you will want to find out what else you can do with a piece of technology beyond the original purpose you had in mind.

TYPES OF TECHNOLOGY INFORMATION SOURCES

There are many avenues for staying abreast of technological change. Following are the most commonly used methods:

Websites and blogs. The **Internet** is a prodigious source of technology information. This information may be in the form of vendor websites, blogs for specific technologies or library systems issues, directories of libraries, product reviews, how-to documents, and technology references.

Electronic discussion lists. **Electronic discussion lists,** including those particular to libraries and those devoted to more general technology issues, can serve as incredible tools for daily updates as well as forums for specific questions. A number of established library lists are devoted to technology questions and answers; others function as services that e-mail daily tips on technology or news related to libraries. Certain sites archive their history of discussion posts to allow users to search for answers to a variety of technology questions.

Periodicals. A number of **periodicals** cover information technology that is pertinent to libraries. Because many kinds of information technology are used outside of libraries, general-interest technology periodicals can be useful resources, as can general periodical indexes and more specific library indexes (such as Library, Information Science, and Technology Abstracts).

Continuing education. Much can be learned from reading blogs and periodicals and searching the Internet, but at times a professional development workshop or class can be even better. For example, you may be able to prepare yourself to work with a given technology by participating in a focused continuing education workshop. Other opportunities may give you an overview of several new technology developments. A large number of workshops and conferences are on offer every year, one or more of which may coincide with your current or future needs for technology information. Attending live, online **webinars** from vendors or library organizations are also a helpful way to gain information without travel.

Conference exhibits and trade shows. Gathering technology information would not be complete without visiting the exhibits at a conference or sampling the wares at a trade show. Attending these events is helpful for seeing what new technologies are available or for quickly comparing a number of similar products. These shows also provide the opportunity to closely examine equipment or software and to ask questions, which is not always possible when viewing web-based information or reading a product review.

Visiting libraries. Finally, we cannot forget the value of seeing technology in the field and communicating with nearby folks who are already using it on a daily basis. Visiting a library that has already implemented the technology you are interested in can give you an idea of how the technology may work in your library. Keeping in touch with a network of local colleagues can help you identify libraries to visit. You can contact vendors and ask for a list of local satisfied customers, or try posing a question to an electronic discussion group for help in generating ideas about local or regional libraries that you can visit. You may find that you can rely on a local or regional library association, or you may need to create an informal group of interested parties to help members keep pace with changes in technology.

SELECTED SOURCES FOR FURTHER INFORMATION

The following list of resources is by no means exhaustive. It does provide some excellent starting places to help you make a habit of staying informed. Look beyond your everyday needs and you will be better prepared for future developments in your own library. Sources are listed in each category in rough order of their usefulness (though your mileage may vary).

Websites and Blogs

TRENDS AND TECHNOLOGY NEWS

Top Tech Trends. http://litablog.org/category/top-technology-trends.
   This is a biannual discussion of technology and library users by the Library and Information Technology Association's Top Technology Trends Committee. These discussions take place at the ALA's midwinter and annual conferences.
Cites and Insights. http://citesandinsights.info.
   This monthly online publication includes in-depth coverage of technology trends written by author and technology guru Walt Crawford. His observations and analyses of recent publications are a must-read!
Seven Things You Should Know About . . . www.educause.edu/ELI7Things.
   Created as part of the EDUCAUSE Learning Initiative, these short monthly pieces provide informative introductions to a variety of technologies (from MOOCs to projecting from mobile devices to the evolution of the textbook) along with possible educational uses for them.
WebJunction. www.webjunction.org.
   This online community bills itself as "the learning place for libraries." Originally funded by the Bill and Melinda Gates Foundation and the Institute of Museum and Library Services (IMLS), WebJunction is now hosted by OCLC. An enormous collection of documents on library technology topics and issues, links to useful websites, discussion forums to find colleagues who have faced (and, it is hoped, solved) the issues you are facing, free webinars, and a host of other resources of interest to libraries. There are also state-oriented versions of WebJunction for eighteen states that combine content from the main website

along with training courses that are offered to library staff via funding sources provided at the state level.

BLOGS

ALA TechSource Blog. www.alatechsource.org/blog.

ALA's site for its technology publications also includes a blog with posts of trends and news in library technology. This team effort of eleven bloggers (plus a growing group of guest bloggers) provides a great overview of library technology happenings combined with helpful coverage of technology events within ALA's divisions.

Tame the Web. www.tametheweb.com.

Tame the Web is a blog written by Michael Stephens, assistant professor in the Graduate School of Library and Information Science at Dominican University in River Forest, Illinois. He shares student projects, interesting discussions, and commentary on the latest developments in library technology.

Digital Libraries. www.thedigitalshift.com/category/roy-tennant-digital -libraries.

Digital Libraries is a blog written for *Library Journal* by Roy Tennant, a senior program officer for library research at OCLC. He writes about all manner of developments in library technology and how they impact libraries, offering his experienced perspective alongside useful links.

Swiss Army Librarian. www.swissarmylibrarian.net.

Brian Herzog authors this blog, which is mainly focused on the work of a public library reference librarian but tends to wander into all sorts of technology directions.

Inkdroid. http://inkdroid.org/journal.

Inkdroid is written by Ed Summers, an information technology specialist and programmer at the Library of Congress. He covers a diverse blend of technology topics, ranging from really involved programming discussions to broad technology introductions.

LibrarianInBlack. www.librarianinblack.net.

This blog, written by Sara Houghton, director for the San Rafael (CA) Public Library, is a very useful site for information on technological issues and trends in libraries.

Disruptive Library Technology Jester. www.dltj.org.

The tagline for this blog reads "We're librarians, we're disrupted, and we're not going to take it anymore." It is written by Peter Murray, assistant director of the Technology Services Department at LYRASIS. Peter uses the blog to explore change in libraries and the technologies they use, both incremental and disruptive.

ResourceShelf. www.resourceshelf.com.

ResourceShelf is a daily updated library blog of "resources and news for information professionals" that presents excellent focus on industry trends and developments in online searching for all library types.

DICTIONARIES AND GLOSSARIES

Wikipedia. www.wikipedia.org.

This collaborative online encyclopedia includes articles on a wide range of subjects. Despite much criticism and discussion of its questionable value as an information source, I find that it has excellent explanations of current technology topics. (But don't just trust me; read them critically on your own.)

Webopedia. http://webopedia.internet.com.

This is a searchable dictionary of computer and Internet technology terms. This very extensive source includes a brief definition for each term along with links to related terms and websites that offer additional information. A number of entries also include diagrams or images.

ODLIS: Online Dictionary of Library and Information Science. http://lu.com/odlis.

This up-to-date dictionary of terms common to the field of library and information science includes a number of entries relating to technology, compiled by Joan M. Reitz.

HOW-TO DOCUMENTS

TechSoup for Libraries. www.techsoupforlibraries.org.

The site includes "cookbooks" on IT maintenance planning and technology planning created as a project (funded by the Bill and Melinda Gates foundation) to compile information on how public libraries support public access computers. TechSoup offers free webinars on various technology issues. There is also a blog that covers recent developments in and discussions of public computing issues. Much here is applicable to various library settings.

Library Success: A Best Practices Wiki. www.libsuccess.org.

This wiki is a collaborative collection of documents and links covering library-related issues of all kinds, with an emphasis on sharing best practices. The section on technology linked from the list of contents has excellent explanations of many library technologies and suggestions on implementing them in your institution.

WebJunction. www.webjunction.org/content/webjunction/explore-topics.html. WebJunction includes a section on technology in libraries that holds useful documents on equipment and planning for technology that may be helpful.

About.com Computing and Technology. http://about.com/compute. This section of the About.com site includes collections of articles and links to additional websites on various technology topics.

PRODUCT REVIEWS AND VENDOR INFORMATION

CNET. www.cnet.com. This site includes lots of technology information, product reviews, how-to documents, and advice. It is the place to start when you are planning to buy computers or other technology items.

ZDNet. www.zdnet.com. A very similar site to CNET, it provides another excellent source for product reviews and buying guides.

Library Technology Guides. www.librarytechnology.org. "The Library Technology Guides website aims to provide comprehensive and objective information related to the field of library automation," according to the website. It is an excellent source of library systems–related reports, articles, and trends. It includes a directory of library system vendors.

Library Resource Guide. www.libraryresource.com. This website provides an annually updated directory of library services and suppliers compiled by Information Today.

The Librarian's Yellow Pages. http://librariansyellowpages.com. This comprehensive listing of library vendors may be browsed by type of product or service or searched by keyword.

MacInTouch. http://macintouch.com. This site provides news, tips, and reviews of Macintosh products and software as well as other Apple products (iTunes, iPhone, etc.).

Individual vendors. Other vendors can also be found through Google (www.google.com) or other search engines.

ELECTRONIC DISCUSSION LISTS

Web4Lib. http://lists.webjunction.org/web4lib (subscription information and archives).

This is a very active discussion list that focuses on web-related technologies in libraries but also discusses other issues including public computer setup, library website design, scanning, and search engine developments, to name but a few regular topics.

LM_NET. http://lmnet.wordpress.com (subscription information and archives).

While this list focuses on school librarians and school library issues, many of the discussions have a strong technology focus (particularly electronic resources and educational technology). Be warned: this is a highly active group.

LITA-L. http://lists.ala.org/sympa/info/lita-l (subscription information and archives).

This is the mailing list for the Library and Information Technology Association (LITA) division of ALA. The list presents a good blend of workshop/conference/job announcements along with interesting technology articles and discussion of questions from list members.

SLA-DITE. http://units.sla.org/division/dite/sladite_new.html (subscription information and archives).

This is the mailing list of the Information Technology division of the Special Libraries Association (SLA). It is a general-purpose list to seek technology recommendations or to discuss new technology trends and developments.

Individual groups.

There are many other library-related electronic discussion groups, including a large number devoted to specific technologies or products. A good resource for finding others is to try a search in Google Groups (http://groups.google.com) to locate other library discussion groups that may be indexed there. A search for your topic (say, "library technology") combined with the word "list" or "discussion group" in a search engine may also prove effective for lists housed elsewhere.

Tips and Trends E-mail Newsletters

LISNews. http://lisnews.com.

LISNews is a blog of library-related news happenings that includes discussions which grow out of the individual postings. You can sign up for e-mail updates of new postings.

Current Cites. http://lists.webjunction.org/currentcites.

This free, monthly e-mail contains annotations of information technology articles and other items written by a team of librarians and library staff. It provides an easy way to scan the professional literature for technology-related publications.

Periodicals

Note: Subscription information is available on each periodical's website.

LIBRARY ORIENTED (TECHNOLOGY FOCUS)

Computers in Libraries. Information Today. Ten issues per year. www .infotoday.com/cilmag/ (sample full-text articles are available).

This publication features articles on applications of computer technologies in libraries and reviews of technology products and has a very practical focus. The "Tech Tips for Every Librarian" column is really helpful.

Information Technology and Libraries. Library and Information Technology Association. Quarterly. Subscription included with LITA membership. www.ala.org/lita/ital/ (table of contents and abstracts are available).

This periodical features articles on applications of information technology in libraries.

Library Hi-Tech. Emerald Group Publishing. Quarterly. http://info .emeraldinsight.com/products/journals/journals.htm?id=lht (sample full-text articles are available).

This publication features articles on emerging technologies in libraries. Although it is a bit more research-oriented than *Computers in Libraries*, it includes a variety of practical case studies as well.

Library Technology Reports. American Library Association. Eight issues per year. www.alatechsource.org/ltr/ (issues are available both digitally and in print).

This publication features extensive reviews, studies, and testing of various examples of library technology items, from embedded librarianship to web scale discovery services.

Online. Information Today. Bimonthly. www.infotoday.com/online/ (sample full-text articles are available).

This periodical includes articles, reviews, and product information on databases and other electronic library resources. It also includes coverage of broader library technology issues, such as e-books.

LIBRARY ORIENTED (GENERAL FOCUS)

American Libraries. American Library Association. Bimonthly. Subscription included with ALA membership. www.ala.org/alonline/ (news stories and some columns, including *Technology in Practice* and *Internet Librarian,* are available in full text).

This magazine for ALA members includes excellent "Internet Librarian" and "Technology in Practice" columns along with occasional technology-related feature articles.

Information Outlook. Special Libraries Association. Eight issues per year. Subscription included with SLA membership. www.sla.org/io (tables of contents for each issue are available).

This publication for SLA members includes the technology column "Info Tech" as well as occasional technology-related articles.

Library Journal. Media Source. Twenty issues annually. www.libraryjournal.com (news stories, articles, and columns are available in full text).

This periodical includes articles on various library topics and it is also noted for its reviews of books and media items. In addition to special articles on technology topics, it includes a number of technology-related columns (e.g., "The User Experience") and regular reports on digital collections and sources.

School Library Journal. Media Source. Monthly. www.schoollibraryjournal.com (full-text news stories and articles are available).

This publication for school librarians includes technology-oriented articles and product reviews.

In addition to the titles mentioned, there are two excellent resources for finding technology information published in other library-related periodicals. The periodical index *Library Literature and Information Science Full Text* (EBSCO Publishing; more information available at www.ebscohost.com/academic/library-literature-information-science-full-text) is the gold standard in its coverage of the library and information science field. *The Informed Librarian Online* (www.informedlibrarian.com) is a unique resource for scanning the monthly output of some 312 library and information-related periodicals. The free version of the service provides a monthly e-mail update to new issues with links to selected items. A premium subscription service provides full access to the tables of contents for the periodicals and adds access to a selection of full-text articles, a searchable archive of past issues, and a search interface to all linked periodical issues.

GENERAL TECHNOLOGY

Though too numerous to list here, a number of good periodicals out there may well help with a particular technology information need. They range from computing periodicals such as *Macworld* (www.macworld.com) or *PC Magazine* (www.pcmag.com) to broader technology titles such as *T.H.E. Journal: Technological Horizons in Education* (www.thejournal.com). These periodicals and others can be reached using any general periodical index to find product reviews or information on a wide variety of technologies.

Continuing Education, Conference, and Trade Show Opportunities

Although there is no comprehensive national or international directory of library continuing education or professional development events, the *Library Conference Planner* website by Douglas Hasty (http://lcp.douglashasty.com) can be very helpful. It lists a large number of national and international conferences to consider, along with the dates for their next meetings. Some state organizations provide calendars for individual states or selected regions. Check with your state library or local or regional library organizations for assistance in finding a calendar of local events. The following resources can help you find events offered by national and international library organizations.

Yahoo! Directory: Library and Information Science Organizations. http:// dir.yahoo.com/Reference/Libraries/Library_and_Information_Science/ Organizations.

Yahoo!'s **search directory** lists various international, national, state, and local library and information science organizations. Look at the websites of these organizations to see what conferences or professional development opportunities they are offering.

Information Today: Events Calendar. www.infotoday.com/calendar.asp. Information Today offers a calendar of major conferences and events in the library and information-seeking world with a worldwide focus.

American Library Association: Affiliates Conference and Event Calendar 2012–2024. www.ala.org/conferencesevents/afficalendar.

This webpage, part of the ALA website, lists conferences and meetings sponsored by ALA and its divisions (arranged by division or by date), along with the scheduled future activities of various organizations.

Special Libraries Association: Events Search. www.sla.org/calendar/ eventsearch.cfm.

This webpage allows users to search a calendar of professional development opportunities offered by the SLA and its chapters.

Find Libraries Near You

While attending a program on a given technology or even visiting a vendor at
a conference can be useful, there is nothing quite like seeing a technology at
work in a library. Aside from just being neighborly and being aware of other
libraries in your area, it pays to know whom to visit to see new technologies
at work. Here are some methods for tracking down local or regional libraries.

American Library Directory. www.americanlibrarydirectory.com.
> This is an invaluable resource for locating libraries in the United States
> and Canada. The print version of the directory may be found in many
> libraries' reference collections. The online version offers a free registra-
> tion option that allows users to search the directory and find library
> addresses.

WorldCat: Find a Library Near You. www.worldcat.org/libraries.
> This webpage presents an advanced search tool for locating libraries
> that are members of OCLC or that have registered (at no charge) with
> WorldCat.

PublicLibraries.com: State Libraries. www.publiclibraries.com/state_library
.htm.
> This webpage offers an alphabetical list of links to state library websites.
> Most state libraries maintain directories of libraries in their state that
> can be searched by location or zip code.

A final suggestion is to post a message to one or more of the electronic
discussion lists mentioned earlier (or those found in the previous directory
of lists). You could ask if there are any libraries near your location that are
already using a given technology.

MODERATION IN ALL THINGS

As information professionals, we are all too aware of the dangers of having too
much information descend on us. This chapter has given you many sources
of information to consult, some as long-term subscriptions and others as
momentary, need-based consultations. Be sure not to let the number of
blogs, discussion lists, and print and e-subscriptions overwhelm you. Choose
a few sources to regularly consult to stay abreast of trends, and then leave

others for future needs. I heartily commend you to read a 2008 article by Sarah Houghton-Jan, "Being Wired or Being Tired: 10 Ways to Cope with Information Overload," *Ariadne* no. 56, at www.ariadne.ac.uk/issue56/houghton-jan.

QUESTIONS FOR REVIEW

1. List three reasons for consulting technology information sources.
2. Do many periodicals have free full-text articles available on their websites? Name two that do offer this service.
3. What methods are you currently using to keep up with technology developments (or other professional happenings) that may affect your job?
4. Find two or three resources in the lists provided in this chapter and try monitoring them for a month. During that time, keep track of useful information you learn. This practice will help you decide whether a given resource is really worth watching.

CHAPTER 4

EVALUATING, BUYING, AND IMPLEMENTING TECHNOLOGY

NOW THAT WE HAVE EXPLORED how our technological world came to be, and now that many resources for investigating technologies and keeping track of their ongoing development are in hand, it is time for a structured look at putting the technology in place. Libraries must determine their technology needs and also which technologies can best meet those needs. Once identified, the next steps are to compare, choose, purchase, and implement the technology. By systematically evaluating the technologies or products, buying them, and then putting them to work, libraries can successfully add the right technology at the right price. It will be helpful to have this process in mind as we explore individual technologies in subsequent chapters.

KNOW WHAT YOU NEED

The first decision to make when adding technology is whether there is a need for it. We cannot evaluate whether a given technology is useful to our situation unless we know what need it is meant to address. Sadly, in some situations a new technology is chosen and implemented as a result of "technolust" (choosing technology for its glitz rather than actual need) and then never used. Start with a need, and then base your evaluation on how well a given technology meets it.

The process of needs assessment is discussed in more detail in Chapter 18 as part of the technology planning process. Here, we consider how we become aware of technology needs, including the following common ways:

Personal or colleague observations. Staff members may notice that too few public computers are available, leaving patrons milling about the reference area while they wait for a computer. Technical services staff may suggest that an additional printer or bar-code reader or computer is needed to make the processing of library materials more efficient. Reference staff may note that providing access to a digital image database would help students with graphic design projects. You might wonder if a new, faster copier would help reduce the wait for patrons who are in line to make copies.

Patron requests. Patrons may ask at the circulation desk for the ability to borrow e-book readers. A faculty member might lobby for a specific database to use in his or her teaching. Patrons might ask when your library will begin to offer downloadable audiobooks or e-books as the library in a nearby city does.

Surveys or suggestion boxes. Compared to the previous two methods listed, in which observations or requests come up in the normal course of business, using surveys or suggestion boxes is a more active method of discovering possible technology needs. Whether a survey is aimed at patrons or library staff, survey results can reveal popular interest in new or updated technology options. Surveys (print, electronic, or both) might be focused on technology or might be more broadly designed to gauge patron satisfaction. As well, more informal electronic suggestion forms or physical suggestion boxes can be used to provide ideas for technology additions to the library or its collection. Libraries are more focused than ever on assessing patron satisfaction—and they should also be concerned with staff satisfaction. Distributing surveys and encouraging suggestions will increase the input that libraries need for various areas of operation.

Keep in mind that the elements of perspective and participation impact the needs assessment process. In terms of perspective, what staff members guess that patrons need might not be what patrons really want. A technology that patrons would love to have may not be economically feasible for the library to provide. Perhaps a submitted idea is of interest to only one person and would not be wildly popular. As far as participation, surveys and suggestion boxes might attract the interested few (or those with something to get off their chests) but not provide a valid view of the wide-ranging target audience's needs, whether composed of patrons or staff or both.

If a particular new technology suggestion would involve a large change in the library's services (such as adding a public scanner or starting an electronic reserve collection), then the groups who are most likely to be interested in or affected by the change should be surveyed or have input on the idea. This is a way of gaining focused responses and brainstorming that can shape the actual technology you choose and how it is implemented. Surveys or questionnaires aimed at patrons can serve to market the eventual adoption of the technology and may prove that the need is stronger than initially realized. At my library, we display whiteboards with specific suggestions of changes we might make and ask patrons to comment on them; we also ask more open questions to gather information on needs we had not imagined were there. Whenever possible, try to build evidence that supports the need so that funding agencies and library administration can create justifications to support budget requests for the technology.

It is also worth considering that sometimes we start with ideas rather than needs. As you develop your habit of watching technology trends, you will run across many technologies that may address a need in your library. However, you may not yet have that need. In such situations, hold on to these ideas until the time is right. Perhaps these methods will help you discover a need that turns your idea from technolust into a valuable solution.

LOCATE AND EVALUATE TECHNOLOGY CHOICES

From our identification of needs, we now turn to the search for solutions. At times, there may be a number of technologies that could meet the need. Sometimes the technology solution is clear, but the individual manufacturer or version still needs to be decided. Chapter 3 offers a number of methods and sources for seeking information and advice on technologies. These sources are likely to prove helpful in locating the right technology or at least providing some possible choices. Consider the following nine criteria when comparing equipment, media, and electronic resources:

Is the technology suitable? Does it really meet the needs that have been identified? The needs analysis should have identified some problems to be solved. Now we need to determine whether a technology or product can provide the solution. If a library wants to lend e-books to its users to download on their mobile devices, it makes no sense to purchase e-books that can be accessed only through a web browser.

Is the technology close to obsolescence? Even if the current technology meets the need, is something better coming along? With all technology we face the issue of it becoming obsolete more quickly than we would like. This question generally forces us into a choice between the new and growing technology and the old and widespread technology. My library is currently facing this question as we transition from lending relatively inexpensive netbooks to full-size laptops and tablets.

How durable is the technology? Can a scanner or copier stand up to heavy use? Can a database provider handle large numbers of users accessing its service? Will iPad or Kindle devices hold up to the perils faced by circulating materials? Technology is expensive, and it should be durable enough to justify its expense.

Does the technology fit into the library's environment? Is the item something that fits the mission of the library? Can a piece of equipment fit into the available space in the library? Some technologies are neat to have but would not advance the mission or goals of the library. This is a checkpoint for assessing whether it is the role of the library to meet the need. I run into this when I consider technologies like 3-D printers: they are very cool and very useful in the right environment but may not yet be essential for a regional campus library.

What implications does the technology have for training? Will the new technology be difficult or easy to learn? Will bringing in this technology seriously affect training services? Sometimes the amount of training required can forestall your addition of a particular technology.

What maintenance, upgrading, or updating needs does the technology have? Are these possible to complete within the library, or will they require outside assistance? Consider workflow—the requirements for staff to interact with the technology outside the information-seeking process. Also consider associated costs beyond purchase.

If the technology has problems, are people available locally (within the library or its community) who can provide support? The technology may be easy to deal with or it may require expertise. If the needed expertise is not readily available, the library must decide whether it is worth acquiring the expertise or if the expense of outside experts is acceptable.

How does the price of the technology compare with similar technologies? What will the total cost of this technology be, both initially and over time? Its ability to fit the need should outweigh discussions of price, assuming the funding is available. Alternatively, sometimes acceptable choices or workarounds to expensive technology are available; another option is that the library's need may have to go unfilled for a while longer.

Is this technology the most appropriate way to provide this information or service? Would another format work better? Ultimately, the library needs to decide whether the technology is really the most suitable choice. This final checkpoint should eliminate nagging doubts if the technology is truly the best option.

THE PURCHASING PROCESS

How purchasing actually flows in a library will differ greatly depending on institutional requirements and processes. Many institutions structure purchasing depending on the amount of money you are spending. For instance, purchases of less than $500 require the use of Form X, whereas purchases of $500 or more require Process Y (and attached Form Z). Any substantial expense, such as migrating to a new library system or choosing among companies from which to lease a dozen copiers, will involve a more formal process than buying individual e-book titles. Decisions that have large, long-term financial implications—such as purchasing a new library security system, placing security tags on the entire library collection, and then regularly purchasing further tags for new acquisitions—may well be made by the library staff alone, even though the library's funding source will see increased demands in the library's supply budget for years to come.

The **request for proposal** (**RFP**) process is commonly used for such large expenses as those mentioned. A request is sent out to vendors who can supply the technological product or products that are desired. The RFP is a document that carefully describes in detail the criteria for the item(s) to be purchased. Vendors, if able to meet the criteria, will respond to the library or its funding agency with a proposal outlining how they will provide what is requested. Often a competitive bidding process is in place to award the contract for purchase to the lowest bidder. At some point within the process, the library is able to evaluate the proposals or bids and decide which one is the best. If by chance the lowest bidder does not meet all criteria, the library can write a justification for selecting a higher bidder and have this decision approved by the funding agency. The RFP process can be very slow and sometimes quite frustrating if no bids exactly fit the criteria. However, it does offer a means to evaluate a **vendor** and justify a decision. Another term for this process is **intention to negotiate** (**ITN**), at least within library database or systems circles. Vendors who respond to an ITN are indicating they are ready to talk details and prices with a library or library **consortium**.

BUYING GUIDES AND TIPS

When ready to purchase, it is vital to keep the following four practices in mind:

Try before you buy. Always find a way to try a technology before implementing it in your library. It is great both to use a demonstration version provided by the vendor and to see the same item in use at another library, if possible. With some tools and products, you can do this in the comfort of your library via the web. Conferences with vendors' exhibits can be a great source for additional browsing and examination.

Compare models and technologies. It is easy to pick the first thing that might work for your situation, but closely examining and comparing several options ensures that you will meet your library's specific needs in the best way.

Know when to buy. As a counter to the last tip, be sure to control your comparison shopping. If you have done thorough comparisons, you should start to be able to see which option is the best; continuing to compare past this point may cause you to unintentionally forestall fulfilling the need that got you started. When you have learned enough, make your decision.

Do not fall prey to myths about technology. There are all sorts of myths out there, but here are a few of the most common: (1) wait before buying—that technology will stabilize eventually; (2) wait before buying—prices for that item will fall before long; (3) wait before buying—that technology is about to become obsolete; and (4) it's cheap and it's here—we'll figure out something to do with it. The first three myths assume that technology changes take place in a defined pattern. Yet technology is always changing; if you follow these myths you will wait forever to find a stable, eternal form of the technology. The fourth myth ignores the hidden costs of any technology. The technology may be cheap initially, but in the long run it will probably cost the library more in space, time, and upkeep and will likely need to be replaced.

IMPLEMENTING THE TECHNOLOGY

Finally, the moment you've been waiting for! The mental image of the technology actually being used in your library provides a powerful vision that can keep you going through all the twists and turns of the evaluation and purchasing process. As the time for implementation arrives, you must be ready for any last-minute obstacles.

Implementation preparations can differ greatly depending on the technology in question and its scope or audience. Replacing a staff printer is a much different process from launching a new time-monitoring system for public Internet computers. Some common considerations, though, can guide your process for starting off a new technology. Consider the following issues:

Installation. Whether or not the technology requires a true hardware or software installation, there will be some necessary process for adding the item to your environment. It might involve planning new loan rules and adding item records for the Nook e-book readers you will now have available for checkout, or testing the new wireless network, or ensuring that the new discovery service can actually run searches on the catalog and your 178 periodical indexes. Some questions that need consideration include the following: Who will handle the installation? Can someone in house do it? What other parts are required (e.g., other technology, furniture)? When will the installation happen? On a related note, is there a deadline of any kind for installation? How can the install be coordinated to avoid delays at heavy use times? Brainstorming about the details involved with implementing new technology can help you better coordinate the activity and avoid pitfalls.

Training. The new technology will not be of much help to anyone unless sufficient training is provided. Training must be planned with the audiences of the technology in mind and must take into account the different levels of ability these groups will need to have with the technology. For example, you would expect that both patrons and library staff need to know the basic operations of your new self-checkout system, but only staff would need to know how to perform troubleshooting on the scanner or how to adjust its on-screen instructions. Although some technological changes (such as replacing common office equipment) may not require lengthy training sessions, be sure to check on individuals' comfort with whatever new technology you implement. Additionally, keep in mind that individuals have different learning styles: a single hands-on session may not be enough. Provide additional sources of information (e.g., cheat sheets, manuals, vendor websites) for later consultation.

Marketing. You need to let people know that the new technology is in place. Some installations provide their own marketing by their physical presence (e.g., "What is that thing next to the reference desk?" or "Hey, my new computer is here!"). Other alterations and additions may not be so obvious. Much could be written about the importance of marketing library services to patrons to increase their use of the library. If the new technology is something that your patrons will use directly, be sure to communicate with them about it.

Assessment. Looking ahead, keep in mind that you will want to evaluate how well the new technology is working in your library. From the beginning of its implementation you can begin gathering a record of successful and unsuccessful interactions. Often a list of this sort can help provide feedback with which to fine-tune the design of user interfaces (e.g., a website or database search screen) or assist in diagnosing technical problems or bugs in the technology or with its installation.

ON TO THE TOOLS!

With the close of this chapter, our foundation for discussing library technology is in place. You should now have an understanding of what technologies have greatly impacted library work, where to find information on these and newer technologies, and how to approach each situation of buying new technology and putting it to work. It is time to proceed with a survey of technology tools which your libraries are already using or which could be implemented soon.

QUESTIONS FOR REVIEW

1. How can you gather input on potential technology needs for your library?
2. Describe the RFP/ITN process.
3. Practice evaluating the addition of a new technology to your library. How would you assess the nine criteria on evaluating technology choices for, say, adding digital audiobooks to your setting? What are the four practices you should follow when buying technology?
4. What issues impact the implementation of new technology in your library?

Selected Sources for Further Information

ALA TechSource. *Library Technology Reports.* www.alatechsource.org/ltr/
index.

This webpage provides access to the archive of past issues of this periodical. Published eight times per year, each issue is dedicated to a certain
technology product or application of technology. These reports offer suggestions on specifications to pay attention to and questions to consider as
you choose a product.

Anderson, Joseph. 2012. "WebJunction's Focus on Buying Hardware and
Software." Dublin, OH: WebJunction. www.webjunction.org/content/
webjunction/documents/wj/WebJunction_039_s_Focus_on_Buying_
Hardware_and_Software.html.

This article provides an overview of the purchasing process, complete
with links to various WebJunction tools and other resources.

Cohn, John M., and Ann L. Kelsey. 2010. *The Complete Library Technology
Planner: A Guidebook with Sample Technology Plans and RFPs on
CD-ROM.* New York: Neal-Schuman.

This manual outlines the RFP process and offers advice and adaptable
forms to use in your preparation of these documents.

Knox, Karen C. 2011. *Implementing Technology Solutions in Libraries:
Techniques, Tools, and Tips from the Trenches.* Medford, NJ: Information
Today.

Concise and comprehensive, this book gives a great overview of the planning process and steps for creating RFPs and technology plans.

Lipinski, Tomas A. 2012. *The Librarian's Legal Companion for Licensing
Information Resources and Services.* Chicago: Neal-Schuman.

With up-to-date references and copyright information, this manual
gives guidance on understanding and negotiating licensing agreements
for software and electronic resources—a crucial issue for networked
resources of all kinds.

Stephens, Michael. 2008. "Taming Technolust: Ten Steps for Technology
Planning in a Hyperlinked World." http://dl.dropbox.com/u/239835/
AzLATecnoPlanning.pdf.

Stephens suggests ten steps for library staff to take to better shape their
choices about technology and how it is implemented and used. This PDF
(based on a slide presentation made to the Arizona Library Association
in November 2011) builds on an excellent article he wrote titled "Techno-

plans vs. Technolust" (*Library Journal*, November 1, 2004, www.library-journal.com/article/CA474999.html). The article cautions against losing focus by following too many intriguing technologies at once.

PART II
TECHNOLOGY TOOLS FOR LIBRARIES

CHAPTER 5

COMPUTERS IN LIBRARIES

DESKTOPS, LAPTOPS, MOBILE DEVICES, AND OFFICE APPLICATIONS

COMPUTERS ARE A UBIQUITOUS feature of society with impacts in every sphere of life. Libraries are no exception: the typical library has computers readily available for library patrons and staff members alike. Even in our highly technological age, an understanding of computers is not a universal skill. The goal of this chapter is to provide essential information to help you understand the basic pieces of a computer and how computers operate. Many of the remaining chapters in the book address more specific uses of computers (for instance, library systems in Chapter 7 and library websites and services in Chapter 13). This chapter serves as a guide to the computer itself and its accompanying technology, as well as provides a list of some common library uses for this technology.

DESKTOP COMPUTER ESSENTIALS

A few basic points should help you understand the makeup of computers. We will discuss various types of computers by the end of the chapter, but let us start with the personal computer (PC) or **desktop** computer. As suggested by the name, this kind of computer typically sits on a desk or table. A desktop computer consists of the **central processing unit** (**CPU**), sometimes called a box or a tower, which is the part that contains the main components of the system; some **input devices**, such as a keyboard and a mouse; and peripherals, which include monitors, printers, and scanners.

Every component in a desktop CPU is plugged into the **motherboard**, a piece of circuitry that serves as the foundation for the workings of the computer. There is a **processor**, which powers the calculations the computer must make to run software and process information. **Random access memory** (**RAM**) also helps the speed and performance of the computer by giving software some space in the memory in which to work while it is running. There are also a variety of **cards** on the motherboard, components that serve specific functions for the computer. These include **video cards**, which allow items to be displayed on the monitor; **sound cards** to control audio output; and modems or network cards that allow the computer to communicate with other computers through a variety of networks. Some of these cards and their functions are built into the motherboard; others fit into slots on the motherboard—being added or changed out as needed.

Space to store information in desktops comes in two varieties: RAM is memory space that can temporarily hold the computing processes spawned by running software; ROM (read-only memory) contains information that cannot be altered by the user. Storage devices of various kinds, the most common of which are listed in Table 5.1, are needed for long-term storage and moving software and other **files** from computer to computer. A **hard drive** typically has the capacity to hold many different software programs and files and serves as an **internal storage device**. **External storage** or removable storage is available in the forms of **flash drives** and **DVD-R/DVD-RW drives** in most current computers; though fewer in number, some desktop computers may have **floppy drives**, **CD-R/CD-RW drives**, and **tape drives**. These options will be discussed further in Chapter 8.

Regarding storage, Table 5.2 contains terms of measurement that are used to express the capacities of computer equipment. Their definitions should help you understand what this equipment can do and how you can compare similar pieces of equipment. For example, capacities of hard drives are typically measured in **gigabytes** today, although some now have single-digit terabyte capacities (1 terabyte = 1,000 gigabytes).

COMPUTER SOFTWARE

The items discussed in the previous section are collectively termed *computer hardware*. **Hardware** includes any physical part of, or addition to, a computer as well as the complete device itself. Next, we consider **software**, the programs that make the computer do what we want it to do (and on occasion things we were not really planning for it to do). A piece of software is also known as an **application** or, from the earlier days of computing, a program. A wide range of types of software is available, from games to educational applications to financial management packages. I discuss software that is commonly used in libraries later in this chapter and in a number of subsequent chapters. One particular type of software to begin with is operating systems.

Table 5.1 Computer storage media and their capacities

Drive Type	Media Type	Media Capacity	Primary Uses
CD-ROM	CD-ROM disc	700 MB	Application distribution and use
DVD-RW	DVD-R or DVD-RW disc	4.7 GB to 17 GB	Application distribution and archival storage
Tape	Magnetic tape cartridge or cassette	Up to several GB	Archival storage and backups
No drive (USB port)	Flash drives	Up to 256 GB	Mobile memory for file storage or distributing and using applications

Table 5.2 Computer-related units of measurement

Unit of Measurement	Definition
Bit (b)	The bit is the simplest unit of computer information; a bit can have the value of 0 or 1.
Byte (B)	Eight bits equals one byte, which is enough memory to represent a single alphanumeric character.
Kilobyte (KB)	A kilobyte is 1,000 bytes, equivalent to a short note on a single sheet of paper.
Megabyte (MB)	A megabyte is 1 million bytes, equivalent to 200 to 300 pages of text.
Gigabyte (GB)	A gigabyte is 1 billion bytes; it is now the most common unit of measurement for hard drive and storage space.
Megahertz (MHz)	Megahertz is the common unit of measurement for the internal speed of a computer's processor.
Bits per second (bps)	Bits per second is the common unit of measurement for data transmission through modems or computer networks.

Operating Systems

An **operating system (OS)** provides the environment in which all other software operates in a computer. An OS is really just a large collection of software that controls how the computer works. It is important to know which OS you are working with so that you can choose software correctly. Operating systems have a number of capabilities. In general, they interface with the applications we want to use and the computer's processor to make sure that the processor completes needed operations and that we see the results. They allow for **multitasking**, the ability to have multiple applications running at the same time and to switch back and forth among them. For instance, you can be connected to the Internet with a web browser and at the same time be using **word-processing software**, moving between the two applications in turn as needed.

Operating systems also provide the ability to change some characteristics of the interface we use to interact with our applications. The **interface** is what you see on the screen and then manipulate using the keyboard and mouse. Operating systems have what is called a **graphical user interface (GUI)** that provides graphical images, or **icons**, on the screen that can be selected and clicked on to run programs or open up additional folders, containing more icons. After years of **text-based** operating systems, the creation of a commercial GUI by **Macintosh** cemented the GUI as the dominant model for an OS.

The world of desktop operating systems today is primarily divided between Macintosh and **Windows** personal computers (abbreviated as PCs, though technically Macs are also personal computers) and their respective operating systems. (Windows holds a distinct market advantage, with around 90 percent of machines running a Windows OS.) However, there are other players in the game, the most prominent among them an open-source OS called **Linux**. Apple (which created the Mac) is now on version 10.8 of its operating system (known as OS X), although there are still Macs around running OS 9 or OS 8. The most current version of Windows (from Microsoft) is Windows 8, which debuted commercially in October 2012, with earlier versions such as Windows 7, Windows Vista, Windows XP, Windows 2000, and even Windows 98 still running. Linux, developed and updated by a growing community of users, comes in a variety of versions or builds. It has made some penetration into the desktop computer market but is still more commonly used on servers. It will be interesting to see how this develops over time.

The Operation of Computers

When you start a computer by pressing its power button and turning it on, it goes through a process called booting up. We might think of this initialization time as an annoying delay before we can actually do something on the computer. When booting up, the computer needs to make sure all of its components are in order and functional (RAM, hard drive, etc.). This initial processing starts the operating system running and gets you to a point where you can choose an application to use. The operating system runs constantly in the background while you are using the computer.

To turn off your computer, it is important to follow the correct shutdown procedure for your operating system. In most computers, this involves selecting Shut Down from a list of options. By selecting Shut Down, you are allowing the operating system to "get its ducks in a row": it can clear out temporary memory space and cleanly shut down parts of its software. Once all of the system's processes have finished their shutdown processes, the computer's power will turn off automatically, in most cases. Some individuals will shut down a computer after completing a task with it; others will leave the computer running continuously. My general recommendation is to minimize any wasted time that it runs (which somewhat increases your electricity costs) but to also minimize the number of times you turn it on or off (which can wear out the switch on the CPU or stress the operating system). In other words, turn on your computer when you arrive at work and leave it on until you are ready to go home or until you know that you will not work on it any longer that day.

On occasion a computer may lock up, in that an application or the entire computer stops working. This can be due to a failure or error in a particular application or within the operating system itself. If you can still use the keyboard to type commands or move the mouse, you may be able to close a malfunctioning application and then reopen it to continue your work. This can happen sometimes if you have multiple applications open (e.g., you are using your word processor and your Internet browser, and the word processor stops responding to your commands but the browser is still active). If the failure is bad enough that using the keyboard or mouse is impossible (i.e., nothing happens on the screen when you type or move the mouse) you will have to reboot the computer to correct the problem.

COMPUTER PERIPHERALS

The term **peripheral** refers to a variety of optional computer hardware items that have specific functions. All of these peripherals plug into the CPU, mostly using **USB** (Universal Serial Bus) ports or connections. Currently, USB ports are the dominant method for connecting peripherals, replacing earlier **parallel** and serial connectors.

Monitors. The most essential peripheral is the **monitor**, which is used to visually interact with the CPU. Today, most are **LCD** (**liquid crystal display**) flat-panel monitors, which have replaced the earlier CRT (cathode ray tube) monitors. A key consideration with monitors is screen size, with physically larger screens giving the user the ability to see more of a document or a website at one time (or to view multiple applications at once). Trends are toward buying the largest screen you can afford to give you flexibility to multitask among multiple applications. Larger screens are also useful for multiple purposes: Internet viewing, playing DVDs from the computer's DVD drive, or watching streaming digital videos.

Printers. In libraries, **printers** are a very common peripheral. They are used to print everything from instructional handouts to budget reports to book labels. They come in three main varieties: laser, ink jet, and dot matrix. Laser printers provide the highest quality of printing by thermally transferring toner to paper, much like photocopiers. They are the most expensive (though no longer prohibitively so) and usually include such additional features as two-sided printing. Dot matrix printers represent the historical beginnings of computer printing and offer relatively cheap printing on form-fed paper. They are typewriter-like devices that use ribbons to print; they are quite slow and prone to paper jams. Ink-jet printers fall somewhere in between the two in terms of cost and quality. They spray ink onto paper to complete the printing process; they result in documents that look similar to laser-printed documents. They are often chosen as a lower-cost method for providing color printing in a library (instead of color laser printers). Dot matrix printers are disappearing from libraries, while laser printers are fairly standard for public and staff use. On the rise is wireless printing, which is more common outside of libraries now but will likely grow, in part to accommodate mobile devices.

Document duplication technologies. Such peripherals include scanners and separate or all-in-one devices that scan, fax, copy, and print. **Scanners** have increased in popularity as equipment costs have decreased and interest in digital images has grown (more on their uses in Chapter 8). Attaching an all-in-one device to your computer provides the ability to (1) scan and store images or paper documents on your hard drive, (2) print and make copies of electronic documents, and (3) scan and fax documents through the phone line. Although buying an all-in-one peripheral may save space and money in some respects, one downside of these units is that, due to the integration of many different functional components, it may be difficult to correctly diagnose a problem and identify a malfunctioning component. Also, the loss of one function on the unit may impair all other functions until repairs are made.

Mice. With the addition of graphical interfaces, mice were introduced to computing. While keyboard commands can be used to navigate a GUI, the **mouse** is integral to the operation of nearly all computer functions. Cabled mice that plug into USB ports in the CPU are quite common. Wireless mice, which transmit signals into the receiver plugged into a USB port in the CPU, are an affordable and durable option.

Multimedia add-ons. Speakers, headphones or earbuds, and microphones may be added to a computer as needs dictate. Webcams for Internet videoconferencing can be useful for virtually attending meetings. Digital cameras for recording still images and video should not be forgotten here, although their use may not be applicable to all library settings.

Bar-code readers and card readers. To assist in the completion of circulation and technical services activities, bar-code readers can be found as both counter-based scanners (as used in retail stores) and as portable wands or pens. Card readers read patron data from a magnetic band on the card.

MINIMUM STANDARDS FOR NEW COMPUTERS

Minimum requirements for computers are always in the eye of the beholder. What I find acceptable might seem paltry to one person and excessive to another. Moreover, the machine's eventual purpose will influence your choices; a public computer can probably make do with less hard drive space than a staff computer, for instance. The following criteria, the most important aspects to consider, may be useful to guide you in your computer assessment and purchasing.

Processor type. A multicore processor is best—for example, at least a dual-core Intel Core i5 for PCs or Macs; a quad-core if you need to do a lot of work with images or video.

RAM. At least 4 gigabytes (GB) of RAM is a good midpoint. In some instances, 2 GB will work with current processors, but who knows what you might need for upcoming software?

Hard drive capacity. For today's desktop computers, at least 500 GB of hard drive space for a staff machine and 160 GB for a public computer is sufficient and affordable.

USB ports. The more available USB ports a computer has, the better. Try to get at least eight USB ports.

Drives. A DVD-RW drive is useful for playing optical media and saving files. It is not recommended to add a 3.5-inch floppy disk drive; you are more likely to use flash drives or online storage.

Monitor. Flat-panel, twenty-inch monitors are a good size. You may want to go larger, depending on your planned uses.

Networking. Make sure an **Ethernet** network card is included. If you plan to work wirelessly, there are specifications for wireless network cards that should be reviewed before purchase.

If the computer you are considering meets these standards, you can safely be happy with it—at least until a faster processor or larger drive comes out at the same price as you just paid. Realistically, though, because we cannot keep pace with technology, these minimums will keep your computer in good order and able to handle software for at least four years. For most libraries, you will need your machine to last at least that long. Buy the best you can afford at any time.

COMPUTERS IN OTHER FORMS

Though different in form, these devices make use of the same computing processes and principles as desktops do. While desktop computers are still present as staff and public computers in libraries (e.g., in instructional computer lab settings), laptops and mobile devices of all sorts are greatly growing in number among patrons and staff.

Laptops

Laptops were developed to take the computer's CPU, monitor, keyboard, and mouse along with you in a single unit. Mobility is the key element of this device, which gives you the freedom to use software applications wherever you wish, given access to power or a long-lasting battery. Gone is the need to be tied down to a desktop. The popularity and affordability of laptops has pushed them recently to hold a larger share of the overall computer market than desktops.

The laptop fits easily on your lap and consists of a bisected, hardened plastic or metal rectangle. An adjustable, hinged LCD screen makes up one half of the laptop and also serves to protect the laptop's keyboard. The keyboard half of the unit also contains the laptop's processor, hard drive, and additional components. A **touchpad** or trackpad, located below the keyboard, offers the user the option of moving the mouse arrow at the touch of a finger; alternatively, you may also plug in a standard or wireless mouse if you wish. USB ports are a must here as well as with desktops, so be sure to get as many as you can on your laptop.

Laptops originally suffered from difficulties in miniaturizing computer components. Early efforts were not very powerful and quite slow in operation and also weighed more than a truly mobile computer should. Recent developments have brought laptops much closer to desktops in terms of processor speed and reduced their weight significantly. Laptops may contain DVD drives, or you can plug an external DVD drive into a USB port. A wide variety of screen sizes are available, roughly from nine inches through twenty inches. Other than their size, they are very similar to desktop machines in their operation and capability. One difference is that laptops may use flash memory storage drives, rather than the mechanical hard drives found in desktops. They typically take up far less space than hard drives and have no moving parts that can fail. These size- and weight-reducing innovations led to the development of the MacBook Air and the Windows laptop category of Ultrabook, which are very lightweight, thin laptops with thirteen- to fifteen-inch screens.

Wireless networks, a development we will discuss more in the next chapter, have increased the mobility of laptops and clearly sets them apart from desktops. A laptop equipped with a wireless network card (essential for all laptops) and in proximity to a wireless network can access the Internet or other networked resources without having to rely on wall plugs and cables. This further freedom gives the laptop new potential in library use, particularly in settings where library users desire the chance to roam throughout the building with laptops (their own or the library's) or where adding **network cabling** is not possible without ruining the library's aesthetics.

Mobile Devices

While laptops can be quite mobile, this category represents an explosion of devices that meld computing power and applications in a small package. There are two main types: (1) **tablets**, which are eight- to twelve-inch-long devices with touchscreens, the ability to run software applications (apps), and on-screen keyboards or detachable physical keyboards, and occasionally with pen-like **styluses** to navigate apps—effectively, devices that are all screen for viewing and touch interaction with apps; and (2) **smartphones**, which are cell phones with Internet access, the ability to run apps, and either on-screen or physically built-in keyboards and input options. Both use flash memory storage drives to store data.

These devices are the result of more than fifteen to twenty years' worth of development, evolving from cell phones that had address books, calendars, and contact lists; to **PDAs** (**personal digital assistants**, a basically dead technology with similar features); and Pocket PCs and other devices that used variations of standard PC operating systems and could run a limited number of software applications. Current tablets also mark the successful outcome of earlier attempts to make a laptop smaller and use a touchscreen (these were called tablet PCs) and seem to sound the death knell of the **netbook**, a significantly smaller laptop with a keyboard. Now they stand as widespread devices with ever-growing functions that library staff should be aware of—and are probably already using. The availability of mobile devices, joined with laptops, moves us toward a world of **ubiquitous computing**. Computers can be ever present with us because they are so easy to take along everywhere we go. A great number of applications and files can be accessed in a device that fits easily on a belt clip or in a pocket or purse.

Smartphones and tablets use a variety of operating systems, some of which are specially created for mobile devices and others which are commonly used in desktops and laptops. Apple has grabbed a large piece of both markets with its iPhone smartphones and **iPad** tablets, both of which run versions of Apple's proprietary iOS. Standard OS choices in smartphones include Android (produced by Google, and now far exceeding the market share that iOS holds for smartphones), Windows Phone 8, and BlackBerry OS (a former major player, but now fading fast). Android, like iOS, is also used in tablets, and Windows 7 is currently featured in some tablets, with growth expected in this area with the recent release of Windows 8. All of these OS choices feature OS-specific versions of apps, a number of which allow for features similar to what you would see on your desktop computer. One final note about these devices is that they come with cell phone access, Wi-Fi access, or both. Cell access can require costly monthly data plans to use the device for web browsing, whereas the ability to use Wi-Fi is cost saving, if you can find a network. Smartphones tend toward having both options available, while tablets have Wi-Fi only. Ubiquitous use is strengthened by being able to communicate from wherever you go that receives a Wi-Fi or cell phone signal.

Where do these devices fit with libraries? They may be used by library staff members to communicate with one another and with patrons, or to provide access to cataloging systems and other web-based resources when working on projects in the stacks or assisting patrons while roaming through the library. But beyond these staff uses, there is staff and patron interest in making e-books available through these devices, among others. There is also the desire for patrons to have mobile access to the library and its databases so that they can run searches. Libraries typically set up their public online catalogs and websites with mobile versions that allow patrons to text call numbers to their cell phones or to browse library resources. If libraries expect these mobile users to depend on their services, they will have to ensure that interface designs are compatible with the smaller screens of these devices. As any computing platform becomes popular with a significant number of patrons, the library must be prepared for the design and service implications that come with that platform.

LIBRARY USES FOR COMPUTERS

Computers have impacted nearly every facet of library operations. Some uses are primarily available to staff members, while others are used by both staff and the library's public. Every day a library somewhere is probably thinking of and adding a new use. At the present time, however, the following are the primary categories of use for computers in libraries.

Collection Organization and Control

Libraries hold the maintenance, organization, and growth of their collections as a major facet of their missions. As such, the areas of a library organization dedicated to these services have been early adopters of computers. In particular, the cataloging, acquisitions, and circulation operations of libraries use library systems or independent pieces of software to accomplish their tasks. The volume of work in these areas, as well as the fact that they each involve tasks with a fairly static, repetitive process, has made them clear targets for automation. Adding records for items to an online catalog, ordering materials from vendors, and tracking circulation and fine information are daily technology tasks in most libraries. Some libraries also use mobile devices for running inventories of their collections.

Interlibrary Loan

The practice of borrowing materials from other libraries and lending owned items existed before the computer age. For interlibrary loan (ILL), the advent of computers has made it much easier to locate libraries that own a requested book, video, or periodical article. Also, electronic management of borrowed and lent items is much more convenient than with paper files. While much of the transmission of materials still takes place through postal services, courier services, or fax, computers have added the ability for periodical articles or book chapters to be transmitted via the Internet. The addition of an inexpensive scanner allows for the digitization of documents and their transfer to a receiving library. Even more common is the sharing of full-text versions of articles via e-mail or other methods. Other libraries use computers or e-readers to share particular e-books they have purchased to fulfill ILL requests—for example, it can be cheaper to buy an Amazon Kindle title than it is to borrow the item from a given library.

Electronic Reference Resources

As discussed in Chapter 2, the ability to access reference and informational resources from beyond the library building strongly impacted libraries during the final quarter of the twentieth century. Libraries are providing periodical and reference databases to their communities both from within the library and from individual users' computers at home or work. The resources themselves are usually not housed in the library but rather on the computers of multiple vendors and consortia. The scope and depth of a library's collection can be quickly multiplied by the addition of these resources, provided they are well chosen.

Internet Access Tool

Providing Internet access to staff and the public is crucial since the Internet has become an important information resource for libraries as well as a medium to connect to electronic resources. Libraries need to provide access in ways that that fit their missions, and for many libraries this means having access to the Internet from a number of public computers as well as from most or all staff computers. Having computers available with the requisite peripherals and speed to handle Internet communication is a must. For a number of people in any community, the local library's access might be the only means available to reach resources on the Internet.

Management/Office Tool

Libraries have elements of work that are no different from any other business enterprise. As such, libraries need to have software that is commonly found in business and home settings. Word-processing applications can be used for the production of handouts, memos, and reports of various kinds. **Spreadsheet software** is useful for keeping track of budgets and schedules. **Database software** is handy for maintaining mailing lists and for creating smaller databases for managing periodicals and other purposes. These software packages are often sold together in combined office suites or as a single piece of software that can fulfill all of the functions described. Microsoft Office (including Word, Excel, PowerPoint, and Access) is by far the most common office suite, although there are some open-source alternatives (OpenOffice is one; see www.openoffice.org). Another heavily used alternative is the web-based set of free office suite applications available from Google Drive (http://drive.google.com). In turn, Microsoft has created Microsoft SkyDrive as a free office suite and storage tool (http://skydrive.live.com).

Instructional Tool

Libraries that have a need for creating instructional materials and presentations will make use of a variety of instructional software. **Presentation software** (e.g., PowerPoint) can be used to create presentations combining text, still images, clip art, sound, and video that can be projected in a classroom. Software such as Adobe Captivate, TechSmith Camtasia, or Articulate can be used to take presentations from PowerPoint, combine them with sound and with video, and create screencasts or video tutorials. These tutorials can be linked to the library's website for patrons to watch at any time. More possibilities for instructional use of software are covered in Chapter 14.

Miscellaneous Library Tasks

Many library tasks can be performed using the software in the previous three categories, but a number of tasks require additional software that will vary from library to library and person to person. Staff members responsible for creating documents for a library's website will have web design software on their computers. Catalogers may have software packages installed to access, edit, and download bibliographic records for use in an online catalog. Libraries may use online calendar software to create schedules for desk coverage or staff meetings. More of this category of software will be explored in later chapters.

QUESTIONS FOR REVIEW

1. Name the components of a computer that reside in the CPU.
2. Describe the difference between RAM and the computer's hard drive.
3. What is a GUI?
4. Describe the key attributes of a laptop, a tablet, and a smartphone.
5. Take a look at a website, computer catalog, or ad for desktop computers. If you wanted to buy a computer with the minimum specifications given in this chapter, about how much would it cost? What additional capabilities would you get, and how much more would you pay, if you bought a computer with better than minimum specifications?

Selected Sources for Further Information

Turn to the resources provided in Chapter 3 to find more information on the topics covered in this chapter. Product information and further computer concept explanations can be located in the websites and other resources listed there or found through search engines.

In addition, you can take a look at the *PC Technology Guide* (www.pctech guide.com) for an introduction and further discussion of PC components and operations. It includes a number of helpful diagrams, reviews, and easy-to-understand explanations. For those interested in Apple information, try the Mac section of *About.com* (http://macs.about.com). It has links to Mac products, frequently asked questions, and troubleshooting information.

Clark, Jason A. 2012. *Building Mobile Library Applications*. Chicago: ALA TechSource.
Clark explores the technological and social contexts for libraries providing services to mobile technology users.
Coombs, Karen A., and Amanda J. Hollister. 2010. *Open Source Web Applications in Libraries*. Medford, NJ: Information Today.
This book provides an overview of open-source software, including Linux, and its applications in various library settings for web hosting, reference and instruction applications, and next-gen catalogs.
Kumaran, Maha, and Joe Geary. 2011. "Digital Tidbits." *Computers in Libraries* 31, no. 1: 11–15, 38–39.
Kumaran and Geary provide a look at several free tools that librarians can use for internal and external communications and organization. This article gives a sense of many activities that librarians now perform on computers.

CHAPTER 6

COMPUTER COMMUNICATION IN LIBRARIES

THE INTERNET, WI-FI, AND E-MAIL

SO FAR WE HAVE DISCUSSED computers and suggested some of the tasks that might be completed with them. Most of these tasks are impossible to complete without a way for these computers to communicate with others in the same library or across the world. **Networks**, large or small, wired or wireless, are commonly used in libraries to provide access to shared resources. They expand the library's collection through the electronic resources they bring into the building, and they ease the work of patrons who use them to reach the library's resources from home. This chapter explains how networks operate and how computers use them to communicate. It is fascinating to see how the interconnection of libraries and the wider world not only leads to the completion of tasks we can readily imagine but also provides new service opportunities that can reach untouched communities of users.

WHAT DO NETWORKS DO?

Networks exist to share resources between two or more computers. In doing so, they enable the users of those computers to be connected in terms of communicating and sharing files. In a very simple network, two computers might be networked together to share a printer. Both computers have equal access to one resource, in this case a printer, and avoid duplication (the need to buy two printers). In a more complex situation, a network may be used to share a printer (or several printers) along with a number of software applications among many computers.

A library may have more than 100 computers that need to be able to access the same set of applications (e.g., an office suite, e-mail software, locally networked databases). Rather than purchasing and installing the same applications 100 or more times, the library can network the various applications on one machine (a server) so that all 100 users can get to it. Networks make it very easy to share files, applications, and devices like printers and scanners. They also make it easy to quickly update the software on many machines at once by installing applications on a network server.

Just to note, network managers have at their discretion the ability to run some software from the network server and install other software locally on a computer. There are times when it makes sense to allow the users of individual computers to control the configuration of software that is installed locally. Moreover, locally installed software will be available for use on that computer even if the network is down.

MAINFRAMES AND SERVERS

Chapter 5 discussed computers first because they are found in libraries in the greatest numbers. Computers that are used to host online catalogs or other networked resources are known as **servers**. In the years before there were personal computers (PCs), large applications such as a library automation system required very large and powerful computers called **mainframes** to run them. Individual users connected to the mainframe through terminals, devices that consisted of a monitor and a keyboard, which were cabled directly into the mainframe. **Terminals** did not have separate CPUs (central processing units) or memory of their own; everything emanated from, and was stored on, the mainframe. As PCs became available in the early 1980s, libraries were able to start moving away from terminals and mainframes toward more functional PCs and servers. (However, terminals were still widely used for many years; as an example, the first library I worked in had terminals through the late 1990s.) Developments in processors and the decreasing prices in computer memory, which continue today, allowed many tasks handled by mainframes to move to network servers that are physically not so different from the size of a standard computer. These servers may be used in huge numbers in tandem to provide sufficient storage and processing for services like Amazon or Google. Mainframes, which have extremely fast processing speeds, continue to complete calculations that are essential to research in science, statistics, and mathematics. (For more information on these supercomputers, see the Cray Inc. website at www.cray.com.)

A server (also called a **network server**, file server, or **host computer**) is where software or other resources are installed that people wish to access over the network. The server will tend to have more RAM (random access memory) and a faster processor than an average computer; specifically how much RAM or how fast a processor depends on what the server is being used for. If a server is used to connect a dozen computers to a printer, it need not have even as much RAM as I suggested for a standard computer (4 gigabytes [GB]) and can run an even slower processor. However, if a server is to be accessed by many individuals through the Internet and is running memory-intensive applications (e.g., sound or video files), it will need a lot more than the minimum amount of RAM and the fastest processor you can afford.

A library server might be used for one or more of the following functions:

- Hosting the library's website
- Hosting the library's automation system
- Serving as a file server for word-processing and other office suite software, along with staff documents and other files
- Serving up other electronic resources or services (e.g., blogs, digitized archival materials, an institutional repository) within the library and to the wider world

A library might have several servers in place to accomplish these tasks or it might not have any servers at all, relying on vendors or free sites to host its materials. Libraries depend on the servers of their vendors to provide resources and services that are not hosted locally. My own library uses space on our campus's **web server** to run our website and uses networked applications from another server for word-processing and other applications. We are connected to servers on our main campus for our library catalog as well as servers at our regional consortium and a host of vendors for our periodical databases and other resources. The demands you place on a server depend on the purposes you have in mind for a network.

NETWORK COMPONENTS

You need a number of items beyond a server to operate a network:

- Network operating system software
- Computers with network interface cards and network software
- Printers or other peripheral devices with network interface cards

- Cabling to tie it all together
- Resources (beyond printers and devices) to share
- Routers and gateways to connect users to other networks (as needed)

Network Operating Systems

A network requires network operating system software of some kind. The operating systems we discussed in Chapter 5 all have networking capabilities as part of their makeup. This means you can run a small network from Windows 8 or Mac OS X without having to add additional software. There are also specialized network operating systems that are designed to handle networking processes and communications (e.g., Mac OS X Server, Windows Server, **UNIX**, and Linux). Whichever option is used, the purpose of the **network operating system** is to make sure that everything connected to the network (computers, printers, etc.) can communicate and that the use of those connected items can be managed.

Network Cards and Cabling

Each computer, printer, or other device on the network needs two items to complete its linkage. There must be a **network interface card** connected to the device and there must be a cabling system in place. The card enables the device to send and receive **data** through the network. The cabling provides a physical link between the devices and the server or servers on the network. There are a variety of cable types and system configurations that a network might use. Some common types of cabling are **unshielded twisted pair (UTP)**, coaxial, and **fiber-optic**.

- UTP is commonly used for networks that exchange data, such as e-mail and web-based resources; Category 5 is a popular standard for UTP.
- Coaxial is used mostly for networks that transmit large files or video; it is most prominently used for cable television networks but also for data transmission through these same networks.
- Fiber-optic cable is a lightweight, extremely well-transmitting cable that is excellent for data transmission. It tends to be more expensive than UTP, however, and figures more prominently in telephone networks that in computer networks. Quite a bit of data is transported through these telephone networks.

HOW NETWORKS WORK

There are three main goals of using a network: security, flexibility, and stability. Security ensures that a particular user can use only the applications or the files they should have access to. Flexibility allows users to sit down at any computer connected to the network, log into the network server, and access the same resources they would at another computer. Stability means that the chances of malfunctions or downtime for the network are significantly reduced.

The network software allows each user to log in with a specific username and password. Different profiles can be set up on the network server so that staff members' **log-in IDs** give them access to different resources (or different levels of access to the same resources) than the IDs that are set up for public computers. For instance, library staff members will have log-in IDs that let them access the management side (circulation, cataloging, etc.) of a library automation system from computers in the staff area, at the circulation desk, and even from public computers. Patrons, however, may have log-in IDs for public computers that let them access only the online catalog. It is fairly common to limit what can be done on a public computer in terms of installing new software or changing system settings.

Another facet of network operating systems is that each computer to be connected to the network needs to have network operating system software installed. This is relatively straightforward if the network operating system of choice is already the main operating system for the computer. If it is not, then an additional software package will be installed to allow the computer and server to communicate. In either case, the computer and its network software need to be configured for this communication to take place. Just to note here, there are methods available to allow computers using different network operating systems (or computer operating systems) to communicate. This is all set up with added applications on the computer. This way, you can have machines using OS X, Windows 8, and UNIX all talking back and forth and sharing the same files, printers, and other devices.

No network will run uninterrupted eternally, but there are ways to increase stability and make users more confident about using it. Redundancy needs to be built into the system so that a malfunction in one part does not stop the entire network. There needs to be another path to follow to keep the network running. One strategy for this is to install a backup server to take the place of a primary server that experiences a hardware or software problem. The switch-over can be made without the user noticing an interruption in many cases. On the Internet, many heavily used websites have **mirror sites**, which consist of a server (or servers) containing the same data or resources as the primary site but located on a separate network. This option keeps the site running for users even if the main site goes down due to server, cable, or other connection problems.

LANS, WANS, ROUTERS, AND GATEWAYS

A **LAN** (**local area network**) is basically what has just been described: a server, some computers, and some cabling. It can involve a dozen computers or thousands of them. Likewise, there can be a large number of servers involved. Typically, a LAN is used by a single library or perhaps a single college campus. The speed limitations of the cabling used for the LAN make it difficult to extend the network beyond a single organization or small geographic area. This is because as more computers are added to the LAN, the cable has to handle more traffic, and the network speed will slow.

In those situations, a **WAN** (**wide area network**) is a better option. If there is a need to extend access to the same resources or applications that are on one LAN to people using a different LAN (as in the case of a company with multiple offices), a WAN can be built with devices that allow communication through existing communications networks, such as the telephone network. **Routers** help exchange information between separate LANs, and **gateways** help translate between LANs that use different communication **protocols** (decided by their choice of network operating systems). WANs can then accommodate a larger number of individual users and bring together many more resources for shared use.

WIRELESS NETWORKS

Wireless networks have grown enormously in popularity and number over the past few years. They use radio signal and infrared transmission technologies to allow computers another way to communicate with other computers and network servers. This allows computers to communicate with servers and other users on networks and exchange information without being plugged in. The wireless network can also support the transmission of print jobs from laptops or other mobile devices to a networked printer. Wireless is seen as a way to augment cabled networks by giving users freedom of movement and libraries flexibility in arranging stations for networked resources. The latter option can help those who are finding it difficult to rewire their library building for a network. A library may use both wireless and cable networked stations in tandem to give users flexibility. Library users can bring their own laptops or borrow them from the library and use them to type papers or do research from anywhere in the building.

A wireless network originates from a device that is plugged into a wired network. One arrangement for a network would have a wired server connected to a wireless router which is further connected to wireless access points (WAPs). The WAPs have antennae on them that send signals to, and receive them from, wireless devices. They also boost these signals to carry them through the area covered by the wireless network. In turn, every wireless device has a wireless network card attached to it. WAPs will be strategically placed throughout a library to achieve a strong signal in all areas of intended use. With the proper equipment, the entire library can be a zone (often called a "hot spot") for accessing online resources.

The other side of this equation is being sure to protect your wireless network from individuals who should not have access to it. Wireless signals do not necessarily pay attention to walls or floors or other physical boundaries that separate the library from the wider world. Although you cannot keep your signal from going out into the street or into nearby buildings, you can force users to log in to access the network or to gain wider access to the Internet. This and other methods of network security are discussed further in Chapter 15.

HOW DOES THE INTERNET RELATE TO ALL OF THIS?

The Internet is the network to beat all networks. It can be seen as a very large WAN. It is the combination of many LANs and WANs spread out worldwide. It uses a special protocol, called **Internet protocol** (**IP**), to make it easy for computers using any network operating system to connect to other servers anywhere. Each server on the Internet has its own Internet protocol number, or address, that allows anyone using the Internet to connect to the server. The Internet also uses a system of **domain names** to give a more memorable look to server addresses. (This system allows users to type in the website address, for example, www.muohio.com, rather than an **IP address**, such as 134.53.7.244.)

The Internet is built on very high speed phone lines that are dedicated to transferring electronic data. These lines are typically OC-3, T-3, T-1, and **56 Kbps** lines. **OC-3** lines are able to transmit 155.52 Mbps and form the backbone of the Internet, quickly transmitting **e-mail** messages, files, and requests to view webpages from an individual's computer to another computer or server. T-3 lines make up smaller pieces of the Internet backbone and can transmit 44.736 Mbps. **T-1** lines can transmit 1.544 Mbps and can be leased by organizations (companies, colleges and universities, libraries, or individuals) that require high-speed connections to the Internet. These organizations can plug a T-1 line into their LAN and provide speedy access to dozens of computers.

The route an individual or a library takes to access the Internet may look like the diagram in Figure 6.1.

What's an Intranet?

An **intranet** is a single LAN (or a combination of LANs) that is not available to the general public over the Internet. It is an internal network that is limited to a particular company or organization. It makes use of web technology and Internet protocols to give an Internet look and feel to the internal network. Some larger libraries or educational institutions may have intranets that allow the sharing of resources and secure information among library staff. Other libraries may simply have sections of their websites that require staff to log in to see internal documents.

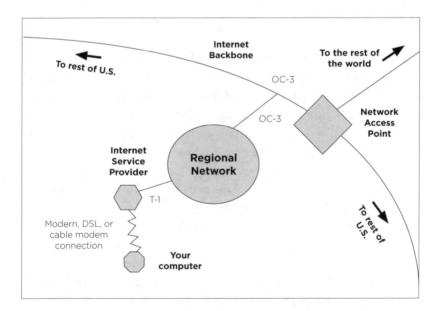

Figure 6.1   Diagram showing how individuals connect to the Internet

HOW TO CONNECT TO THE INTERNET
AS AN INDIVIDUAL OR A SMALL LIBRARY

There are two common options for providing Internet access beyond using leased T-1 lines; these same options are those available to home users. The two have nearly fully replaced the longtime method of using a **modem** to access the Internet through dial-up service. They are often called either **high-speed** or **broadband Internet access**.

ADSL (asymmetric digital subscriber line) is a very fast method for connecting to the Internet using existing copper telephone lines. ADSL is commonly referred to or advertised as DSL, which is a family of communications technologies of which ADSL is only one example. It requires a special ADSL modem, which allows a computer to achieve access speeds between 256 Kbps and 9 Mbps, depending on the individual's distance from the telephone exchange. The service is offered through local or regional telephone companies as well as other **ISPs (Internet service providers)**. Speeds vary widely but are often in the 800 Kbps to 2 Mbps range.

Cable modems use the **coaxial cable** laid for cable television transmission to provide users with access speeds up to 5 Mbps (1 Mbps is probably more common). The modems are connected to the home's incoming cable line as well as to the user's computer. Local cable companies, who own the coaxial lines, offer this service as either a free-standing service or as an add-on charge to monthly cable bills.

Both of these technologies are somewhat limited in use because some areas do not have the infrastructure to support either ADSL or cable modems. Rural areas without cable of any kind or limited phone lines may not have either option. For the individual subscriber, the two options are also quite a bit more expensive than dial-up Internet access. However, you do get what you pay for; for those who choose these options, they provide very fast Internet connections, in some cases equal or superior to a T-1 line.

LICENSING AND PATRON AUTHENTICATION

A huge issue in all this sharing is making sure that the right resources are shared with the right user (or the right number of simultaneous users). The agreements that libraries sign with database providers are designed to ensure that only the patrons of the library are allowed to use the resources. Some licensing agreements also limit the number of individuals who can simultaneously use a database. Libraries tend to offer their resources freely to their communities, and this extends to the many electronic resources they make available on their websites: library catalogs, collections of links to Internet sites, library tutorials, and other documentation. When it comes to periodical databases and electronic reference tools, libraries need to draw the line at remote access to these services.

There are a variety of ways to conform to licensing agreements and provide patron **authentication**, ensuring that only current patrons of a library are accessing a given resource. These options can be divided into one for users within the library and the other for those outside of the library. The outside or **remote access** option requires patrons to log in if they are accessing these resources from home or elsewhere outside of the library. This is pretty flexible in that users can connect to the library's website from any computer and click on the resource to have the opportunity to log in. Or, in other systems, users can log in once upon entering the library's site to gain access to the entire suite of protected resources. The main downside in either case is that people then have to remember a log-in ID and password, and the library has to make sure that it regularly updates its database of valid users. That database may take the form of a **proxy server**, which passes along a user's authentication to any electronic resources included in the server's settings.

Internal authentication of library users is provided by setting up a range of IP addresses with a database vendor. The addresses have been assigned to all computers in a library or an educational institution. Anyone who tries to access the database from a computer with the correct IP addresses gets in; all other users are kept out. This is easier for users in that they do not need to remember log-in information to get access. It also works well for libraries with many different computers in house.

Libraries of all kinds must find ways to make their electronic resources available to their patrons, whether in the library or at home. License agreements are generally written to provide for remote access by users, and then the question becomes a technical and educational one for libraries and their patrons. There are many successful examples of individual libraries and library consortia that continue to make remote access work.

CLOUD COMPUTING

One last aspect of computer networking bears mentioning in this chapter, as it undergirds many of the services that will be mentioned in forthcoming chapters: **cloud computing**. The concept of networking "in the cloud" means that individuals and libraries are relying on software and file services that they access through their web browser (rather than as an application installed on a local network or on a hard drive). This is networking taken a step further, where files and the means for creating and editing them all sit on the web somewhere and can be accessed by end users with a variety of devices. The availability of huge data centers (collections of servers) created by Amazon and others provides the storage space needed. Free services such as the Google Drive and its associated Google Docs office suite are an example of the creative tools and file-saving space that make the cloud work.

QUESTIONS FOR REVIEW

1. Name four tasks or services that libraries make possible using communications technologies.
2. Explain what a LAN, a WAN, an intranet, and the Internet are.
3. What are the pluses and minuses of a wireless network when compared to a cabled or wired network?
4. How does your library connect to the Internet? What Internet access options are available in your area?
5. What are the required parts of a network?
6. What is cloud computing?

Selected Sources for Further Information

Breeding, Marshall, and Ellyssa Kroski. 2012. *Cloud Computing for Libraries*. Chicago: ALA TechSource.

Breeding and Kroski have written a helpful exploration of cloud computing and how it may be applied in libraries.

Caluori, Robert A. 2011. "Chapter 4: Successfully Planning a Scalable and Effective Patron Wireless Network." *Library Technology Reports* 47, no. 6: 29–32.

Caluori's article offers explanations of wireless networking equipment and practical advice on its installation.

Courtney, Nancy, ed. 2010. *More Technology for the Rest of Us: A Second Primer on Computing for the Non-IT Librarian*. Santa Barbara, CA: Libraries Unlimited.

This recent book includes helpful chapters on cloud computing, authentication, and related concepts.

CHAPTER 7

WHITHER THE LIBRARY CATALOG?

LIBRARY SYSTEMS, DISCOVERY LAYERS, AND OPEN-SOURCE OPTIONS

IN THE PREVIOUS TWO CHAPTERS, we have examined the hardware and network infrastructure that libraries need to function in today's technological environment. Our attention now turns toward software that makes the library's internal functions and external services possible. Software (applications or programs) was defined in Chapter 5 as items that make computers do what we want them to do. That chapter discussed operating systems, the elemental software for a computer, and much of the basic productivity software that library staff members use. This chapter introduces integrated library systems, equally the most elemental software for library operations.

LIBRARY SYSTEMS

Library systems software was devised to computerize a variety of library operations, including materials check-in, cataloging, circulation, purchasing, and the online catalog (also known as an **online public access catalog** or **OPAC**). The process of converting these functions to a computerized medium is referred to as library automation. This conversion movement, beginning in the 1960s, opened up a software market aimed at libraries, permitting the purchase of individual modules (e.g., a stand-alone circulation system) or all of the modules combined into a suite, referred to as integrated library system (ILS) software. The advantage of opting for an ILS product is that commands and routines are standardized throughout all the modules, and the modules can cross-reference data from other modules. Today, ILS products are often augmented by modules from other vendors that are (it is hoped) compatible with the ILS. Library systems are not found in every library, but thousands of libraries are using them throughout the world. Small libraries with collections in the hundreds of items probably do not require an automated system. Libraries larger than this should have or intend to implement an ILS of some kind, budget permitting.

A huge impetus for the movement to library systems was the Online Computer Library Center (OCLC). Library systems are highly dependent on machine-readable cataloging (MARC) records, each of which contains a number of fields full of information about an item in the catalog. These electronic records are not created by individual libraries as they need them. Rather, they are largely available from bibliographic utilities: companies that maintain large databases of MARC records and make them available to sub-scribing libraries. OCLC was the original **bibliographic utility**, encouraging its member libraries to contribute their MARC records into a central database for all to share. OCLC provides a variety of services to libraries, but its cen-tral purpose is to maintain a huge computer database of MARC records for print, recorded, and electronic items. These records continue to be created when items are purchased and cataloged by the Library of Congress and the other member libraries of OCLC. Libraries contribute their records to the database and then are able to copy them into their online catalogs. It is a sub-lime example of cooperation. Through the WorldCat database (available in a public interface at www.worldcat.org), OCLC's member libraries keep track of millions of published items and share information about them.

WHAT IS A DATABASE?

To understand the magic of an automated library system (and many other library resources), it is good to have a sense of what a database is. Databases consist of a collection of records, each of which is made up of a number of **fields**, each of which contains a piece of information. Databases meet a very serious need: to organize information in such a way that it can be easily searched and retrieved. Computerized databases exist for all sorts of different functions, from managing mailing lists to helping people find full-text periodical articles.

In a bibliographic database such as OCLC, each record in the catalog con-tains a standard set of categories of information: author, title, publisher, for-mat, subject headings, call number, etc. These categories serve as fields, which can contain whatever information is needed to describe the item. A database is built on the premise that you can find the individual records you need for a given purpose, just as print catalog users once used individual cards to find books or other items in a library. Databases can also be searched by selecting certain fields, much as a catalog can be searched by author, title, and subject. Here is where an electronic database is much different than a print catalog: there is greater flexibility in choosing among fields to search, and there is usually a **keyword** option available that can search across multiple fields at once.

TOOLS FOR THE TRADE

Library systems may be integrated, nonintegrated, or stand-alone. An example of an integrated system would be one that has a **module** (or software program) to handle an online catalog, another module to handle circulation, a third module for managing acquisitions, and a fourth for cataloging new items. All four of the modules work together and share data among them (i.e., the online catalog shows when an item is checked out using the circulation module); this is also called a multifunction system. Most integrated systems are bought as turnkey systems, with all of their modules developed by a single vendor. A **turnkey** is a technology that is set up entirely by the vendor, meaning that you have only to "turn the key" (i.e., press the power button) to start it up.

The nonintegrated library system might start out as an integrated one. The library begins with a system from a single vendor but realizes there are tasks this vendor cannot solve with its system—or that other vendors can solve more cheaply or effectively. Rather than stick with the modules a single vendor offers, many libraries have chosen to add tools such as **electronic resource management systems** or metasearch (the ability to search multiple electronic resources at once) produced by other vendors. The systems can work together from a communications standpoint, but they are not designed to be parts of a larger whole. While in the early days of library systems it was unthinkable (or perhaps impossible) to proceed with a hybrid system, today the interoperability of systems makes nonintegrated systems a reality. Some have forecast the end of the single-vendor integrated system as libraries can now turn to a palette of compatible modules from various vendors. Not to be lost in this discussion is the added time needed to plan and test the operations of the nonintegrated pieces.

A **stand-alone system** would be one in which there is perhaps just a single module or a combination of integrated (or nonintegrated modules) that are not networked beyond the confines of the system. This situation may be found in smaller libraries that have automated more slowly, adding, for example, circulation management first and then deciding to add an online catalog later. Stand-alone systems as a whole tend to be a creature of smaller libraries, where the system runs on a small number of computers on a local area network (LAN), or perhaps just a single computer. They typically lack features and functions that larger libraries would require but can be quite developed and are certainly affordable options.

LIBRARY SYSTEM COMPONENTS

A library system contains a number of different modules. Each is designed to handle or provide a different task or service. Not every system will have each of the following modules, but the five discussed here are the most common ones you will find among integrated library systems.

Online Catalog

The online catalog is probably the most well-known of the modules because it is where the public interacts with the library system. It allows patrons to search a library's collections. For this reason, the design of the online catalog's interface (how one interacts with and navigates the catalog) is crucial. Catalogs offer a web-based interface (or graphical user interface [GUI]) that can be modified to fit the needs and look of a given library. Integrated systems often have some limitations of editing and functionality that can be changed only by working with the vendor and awaiting upgrades. The catalog is generally linked from the library's website and can also be made available through a mobile version.

Cataloging Module

The cataloging module is used to add and modify MARC records for the online catalog. Each time a new item is added to the collection, a MARC record for it must be included in the catalog. The records can be created from scratch within the cataloging module or they can be purchased from a MARC vendor (such as OCLC) and then altered to meet local needs. The first option is known as **original cataloging**, where a skilled cataloger examines the item and enters author, title, and publication information into the system and creates meaningful subject headings. The second option is generally known as **copy cataloging**, where the copied MARC record requires only the addition of a local call number and perhaps other minor modifications.

Acquisitions/Serials Modules

These two modules are actually separate parts of a library automation system, but their functions are rather similar. The acquisitions module is used to electronically order library materials from vendors and then check them into the system as they arrive. The serials module has a check-in function for periodicals that helps the library staff keep track of received and missing issues. The module can also generate claims requests to vendors for these missing issues, as well as routing slips to move selected periodicals among library staff members or groups of patrons (such as college faculty members). Both modules can aid library staff in gathering statistics (number of items or periodicals available in a given subject area, for example) and in financial management (generating up-to-date acquisitions budget figures). These tasks are much more difficult to accomplish in a paper-based system.

As an adjunct service to library systems, libraries have turned to electronic means to select and purchase items for their collections. The process of ordering books and other materials from vendors has automated over time along with other library services. Vendors today are providing sophisticated,

Figure 7.1   Screenshot of a Web-based online catalog

web-based systems for browsing through their catalogs, setting up **collection development profiles**, and placing orders. These systems can be used by single or multiple users at an institution. Faculty members at colleges and universities can even make suggestions for purchases. Some examples of these systems are the GOBI (Global Online Bibliographic Information) system of YBP Library Services (www.ybp.com/gobi3.html), Baker and Taylor's Title Source (www.btol.com/ts3/), and Follett Library Resources' TITLEWAVE (www.flr.follett.com/login/). Except for GOBI, all of these services are available for free registration. These systems stand in addition to long-standing (and now electronic) sources such as Books In Print (www.booksinprint.com/bip/) and web-based book and other materials vendor Amazon.com (www.amazon.com), which is widely used for library ordering and has a book-processing service (www.amazon.com/libraries).

Circulation Module

The circulation module handles the many routine operations of the circulation services department. It can be used to check materials in and out and maintain a record of when items are due. If a patron wishes to place a hold on an item or have an item recalled from another patron, the system can make note of the request and send out recall notices. The module tracks overdue fines and damage charges and can generate bills for patrons. It can also generate overdue notices to mail to patrons. As with the other modules, the circulation module keeps statistics on the number of items circulated and can keep track of circulation by material type and subject area. Circulation modules allow library staff members to replicate their circulation policies in automated form and have the system automatically set due dates, accept holds, and accomplish other routine tasks.

DANCE OF THE MODULES

It is important to understand how these modules interact to make the whole system work. Each module has its own focus, or view, of the overall library system, but an action taken in one module has an impact in other modules. The library system relies on a unique multiple database structure that allows a change in a single item record or patron record to automatically update other records. For instance, when a library patron checks out a DVD, the individual's patron record is updated to indicate that the item is in his or her possession and is due back on a certain date. At the same time, the item record for the DVD is updated to indicate that the item's status has changed (the DVD is no

Figure 7.2   Screenshot of a circulation module interface

longer available and is checked out). This altered status will then show up in the OPAC when another patron searches for the item and locates its record. Similarly, when periodicals are checked in to the system, a notation is made in the check-in record to show that a given issue is now present in the library. This change cascades to a serials holding record and then is visible as an item record for the periodical in the OPAC. This interactivity eliminates much duplication of effort and makes a library system an extremely powerful tool.

NONINTEGRATED MODULES

In the earlier discussion of hybrid systems, I mentioned modules that might be added to an integrated system. Following are brief descriptions of four modules that libraries might add on in addition to the ones already mentioned:

> *Electronic resource management systems.* These systems are used to help the library keep track of its electronic subscriptions to periodicals and other online resources.
> *Metasearch.* Adding on a metasearch module allows library patrons to search the OPAC, periodical indexes, and other electronic full-

text sources from a single search page (as is discussed more fully in Chapter 9).

OpenURL link resolvers. Modules of this type help users identify when their library has the full text of a given periodical article available (again, more on this subject in Chapter 9).

Digital library products. Software modules that help libraries manage their collections of digital items (whether they are text documents, images, video, audio, or combinations of those) are known by the generic term digital library products.

BENEFITS OF LIBRARY SYSTEMS

Library systems provide a number of improvements to library service:

- The system provides users with a wide variety of ways to search for items at the library—both traditional, physical sources and the vast array of electronic reference sources, full-text periodical titles, and e-books that libraries are starting to amass. **Keyword searching** is probably the most obvious addition to the palette once provided by the card catalog, but the ability to search by call number or **ISBN** can be very handy. The more access points you have to a collection of information, the better your chances of finding what you need.

- An online catalog can motivate patrons to use the library more often—or at least attract them to use the catalog, where they may find a larger number of helpful items.

- An online system can help create a technologically savvy image for the library.

- A library system can allow users to access the catalog remotely rather than just within the library.

- Most systems have the ability to link from the catalog to additional electronic resources (periodical indexes, e-books, etc.). This ability allows for the various electronic resources of the library to be integrated into the catalog.

- Once all of the items in the collection have been added to the system, it is much easier to inventory the collection and provide accurate counts of holdings by subject or type of material.

- Many routine tasks are eliminated or made easier by the addition of a system. One outcome of this benefit is that books and other materials may well end up on the shelf more quickly.

As with anything, there can be drawbacks to a library system. The time-consuming, labor-intensive process of converting from a paper-based to an online system is the primary one. But once the switch is made, the benefits will certainly outweigh any ongoing disadvantages. No library completes the difficult and expensive process of converting to an online system only to find that the benefits are not enough for them. It is true that some collections can acceptably be left in a print catalog environment, but these are usually very small, very specialized ones. What I hope to see is smaller libraries joining in cooperative efforts to convert to a library system as a library consortium, distributing any temporary disadvantages among the various consortium members.

OPEN-SOURCE SOFTWARE

Open-source software (OSS) has captured the attention of information technology users from across the spectrum. In general, OSS offers the promise of easily adaptable software applications that are generally free or low cost initially. The second part of that statement is often misunderstood, but the flexibility of OSS is key to its definition. OSS is created by a collaborative group of individuals who then distribute the source code to other programmers for them to use or alter. Individuals can use the software as it is or they can change it and then communicate those changes back to a worldwide community of users and programmers. The hope is that the software will be improved more quickly than a commercial product could be, given that anyone with the ability and interest can innovatively improve it and share in the innovations of others.

OSS is often thought of as free software, and that is usually interpreted as free of charge. Two interpretations of "free" are at work here and are often differentiated using the metaphors "free speech" and "free beer." The "free speech" interpretation of OSS means that no one really owns the source code of the software, and everyone should have access to it in order to make improvements. Once a programmer makes improvements, however, that individual is able to sell the improved version of the software if he or she wishes. The "free beer" interpretation means that the software, its source code, and all later versions should be free for the taking forever. The originators of the open-source movement appear to have had "free speech" in mind as their operating plan, while others in the programming community preferred "free beer." Generally, "free beer" has won out because the source code for most open-source applications (all versions outstanding) is freely available in both the intellectual and economic senses. However, the Linux operating system, an early success of open-source efforts, hews to the "free speech" side: some of its versions are available at no charge, but many users install Linux from versions that are sold commercially.

How is OSS used in libraries? Many library staff members use the Firefox web browser (www.mozilla.com) on their public and staff machines. A number of libraries use Linux on their servers or computers. Quite a large number of library websites run on the open-source Apache server software (www.apache.org). A variety of projects either have been completed or are under way to create open-source library systems (more on this in the next section). Other projects include digital image archives, virtual reference software, and electronic reserve packages. The promise of adding needed technology to a library without incurring substantial expenses will keep library staff watching and participating in the open-source movement for some time to come.

WHERE DO LIBRARY SYSTEMS STAND TODAY?

Library systems have a long history, and some would say that history has brought us to a period of entrenched vendors and stalled innovation. There is a swell of discontent among library staff with the state of the library catalog and much desire to shake up the current order to better serve library patrons. Three major questions are currently being discussed, with a variety of actual progress made for each.

Will Open-Source Systems Make Innovation in Integrated Library Systems Possible?

As mentioned, open-source software is attractive because it involves a product developed by the community that can be further modified and supported by individuals within that community. Library staff find themselves in a world of library systems vendors in which change is incremental and comes at a high price. Open-source library systems have been developed to let innovation run more freely, though the entire process is far from free. Libraries must still maintain the systems and keep staff employed to make adjustments, but the idea is that this is a small price to pay versus the typical route of paying vendors for the initial installation and then annual maintenance fees (plus local maintenance fees and staff time).

Several options exist for open-source systems: Koha (www.koha.org), Evergreen (http://open-ils.org), and OPALS, the Open-Source Automated Library System (http://help.opalsinfo.net), are some established examples, with Koha having the most installations in place. They offer the ability to customize the public catalog side of the operation immensely, adding book cover images, **faceted browsing** (the ability to limit your search by subject heading, date, location, or item type by clicking these choices from a menu on the search results page), and relevance ranking in their searches. Some lack a few of the standard modules we might expect in a library system, while others have built full-fledged ILS examples that are up and running. Adoptions are on the rise, and while the initial answer to this question is yes, only their continued acceptance can put their ability to maintain innovation to the test.

Will a Discovery Layer Interface Make the Catalog More Approachable?
A **discovery layer** is an adaptation of the standard library catalog interface that brings in something of a Google-like simplicity along with a broader reach into information resources. The idea behind it is that library catalogs have become less than approachable to patrons, who would rather use Google to find information. What can be done to reverse this? The discovery layer approach involves moving to a single search blank for users to enter their searches, applying book cover images, faceted browsing, and relevance ranking on the results page, allowing users to tag individual items, and adding in resources beyond those typically found in the catalog (such as results from periodical databases, electronic reference sources, and web search engines).

The overall impact is one that can be more appealing to patrons and more inclusive of the vast information resources available through the library, both licensed and free. Both major ILS vendors and open-source options are available to place a more attractive front end on your existing library system, the back end of which remains in place. Innovative Interfaces offers Encore (www.iii.com/products/encore.shtml) for its Millennium ILS. The Summon Service (www.serialssolutions.com/en/services/summon) is available for sale by Serials Solutions to add onto many existing systems. EBSCO Discovery Service (EDS) (www.ebscohost.com/discovery) can likewise be incorporated in a variety of settings. OCLC offers WorldCat Local (www.oclc.org/en-US/worldcat-local.html) as its ILS add-on, and Ex Libris has a product called Primo (www.exlibrisgroup.com/category/PrimoOverview). On the open-source end, you can see VuFind (www.vufind.org), Apache Solr (the code is at http://lucene.apache.org/solr/; a working example is at http://discovery.coloradocollege.edu/), and Blacklight (http://projectblacklight.org/). The move is on to change the look of the standard catalog.

Figure 7.3   Screenshot of the Colorado College Library Faceted Catalog

Do We Really Need a Catalog?

Even if the look is changed and the content is broadened, some ask whether this whole catalog idea is one that should endure. The argument goes that catalogs came into being to enable a library's owned items to be organized and searched. There is no question that this invention, starting with the card catalog and moving into the online variety, has helped patrons discover information and locate books and other materials. It is also likely true, though, that the catalog may be something built more for library staff than for those who use the library. Do our patrons overlook the catalog because it shows only what we (and possibly our consortium partners) own? Do they turn to Google because it shows them a wider swath of information? Do libraries ignore the larger world of information by concentrating on cataloging only what we own (both physical and electronic) and some selected free e-resources?

Looking back, there was a move to try to catalog the web (or parts of it) and bring sites into the system alongside our traditional library resources.

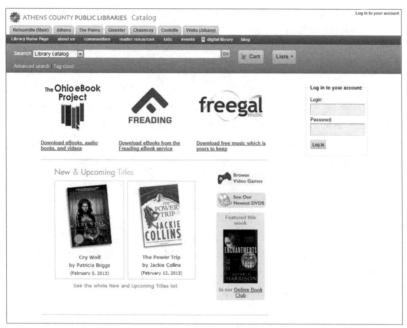

Figure 7.4 Screenshot of the Athens County Public Libraries' implementation of Koha

Since that failed (due to the immensity of the web) and our resources have grown more and more digital, we now face a catalog that is unable to be completed—and is unable to compete with Google and other search engines. Maybe the separate catalog should fade away, at least in today's predominant form. Having a more holistic view of information (not as tied into location or holdings) might be a reasonable plan. Somehow, though, there must be a way to tie our cataloged information into a metasearch engine along with periodical articles and other digital resources, and have one of the new discovery layer options become the new standard interface for libraries.

QUESTIONS TO ASK BEFORE PURCHASING A SYSTEM

Life is full of questions to answer, and the process of purchasing a library system is no different. Consider the list of following options before you buy.

> *How big is the collection?* The answer to this question can have a number of effects. First, if your collection is fairly small, you may not really need an automation system to begin with (or implementing such a system may be more trouble to set up than it is worth). Second, the size and complexity of a collection can impact the vendor or open-

source product you choose. Some systems can only handle a small threshold of items, whereas others are unlimited in their capacity. You need to take your future growth into consideration here as well.

How many users will there be? This question will help you decide whether a stand-alone system on a single computer (with no other online catalog access) will do or if you expect many simultaneous users. Simultaneity and remote access to catalogs are generally givens, but there may be cases where a more limited system will work. If you do expect to have more than a single user, you can then decide the networking setup you will need and also how many computers you should purchase for in-house use. Be sure to think about how many computers you will need for staff use, including machines at the circulation desk or other service points. For public computers, the total size of your library's community should be considered, rather than just the number you expect will be in the library at any given time. The answer to this question will also impact remote access, as will be discussed later.

Which modules are needed? Decide which operations of a library system are needed by the library. You may decide cataloging and circulation are essential but your existing acquisitions procedures would not transfer well to a particular system's environment. Or you may decide that a fully integrated system is the only logical choice. Or that you'd like to build up slowly using an open-source product.

How many remote access users should you prepare for? Remote access is an expected way to use library catalogs. Given that online catalogs are typically web based and are not restricted only to logged-in users, there are few barriers to getting into your catalog. The number of simultaneous catalog users can affect the network configuration you use and the power of your server. This is worth discussing with the vendors you are considering or staff members from other libraries to learn from their experiences.

How long will it take to convert the item records for a collection from cards to MARC records? This is a process known as a **recon**. It involves either keying records from scratch based on the information available on hard-copy indexing cards or copying cataloging records from a bibliographic utility. This is something that the library automation vendor can do for you. However you do it, it is bound to be expensive, time-consuming, and possibly quite frustrating. Just keep telling yourself it is absolutely necessary if you would like to have a working system, and do all you can to exert quality control.

Will you weed before converting? This is a question of process that can have financial implications. As one option, you can convert your entire collection to the new system and then weed out unneeded titles as necessary in the future. However, some libraries decide it is worth their while to undertake a major weeding in advance of a recon so that they save time in conversion. To weed or not to weed becomes part of the planning process for moving to a new system.

Are you migrating to a new system? What will it take to do that? In this situation you already have a working library system and are moving to a new vendor's system. This is becoming a more and more common situation as most libraries already have systems in place and are either switching systems or upgrading to new systems from their current vendors. Here you need to know how well equipped the vendor is to make this transition for you. Have they ever migrated from your existing system to theirs before? The nice part of this situation is that you already have electronic records for the items in your collection. The potential downside is that some records could be lost in the transition.

Can the user interface of the catalog be modified? How freely can you alter the appearance of online catalog screens? Can you change help screens to meet local needs? It would be nice if you had full freedom to rearrange screens at will and easily develop additional types of searches to meet your needs. Some systems have major limitations in how modifiable they are. The best you can hope for is some ability to arrange screen items to your specifications and to adjust the help screens. In other cases, you can make extensive edits and design choices.

Is the staff interface acceptable? We cannot pay all of our attention to the patron interface without thinking of the view that staff will have of the system on a daily basis. Modification may or may not be possible. Still, you need to see whether the work that staff will use the system for (cataloging items, checking out items) can be easily accomplished without extra steps. Then you can compare the process in one system to that in another. Also, is help information easily available? Online help has its ups and downs, but its availability can be more convenient than tracking down the requisite volume of the vendor's automation manual.

What are the future plans of your system vendor? The world of library systems is a fluctuating one. Vendor changes, mergers, and the rapid pace of technological change makes it difficult to assess what the next five years, let alone the next six months, will bring. As you compare vendors, be sure to look at their track records and at their strategies for the future. A number of libraries and library consortia tend to stick with a single vendor or system for a long stretch, putting off a major change process for as long as possible.

QUESTIONS FOR REVIEW

1. What brand of library system has your library chosen? Are you happy with its capabilities?
2. Name the common modules in a library system.
3. What is an important characteristic to consider about both the staff and patron interfaces in a library system?
4. What kinds of software do you regularly use in your work?
5. Explain what open-source software is.
6. What is a discovery layer?

Selected Sources for Further Information

Blyberg, John. 2007. "Mouse Bites Cat: Taking Back the 21st-Century ILS." In *Information Tomorrow: Reflections on Technology and the Future of Public and Academic Libraries*, edited by Rachel Singer Gordon, 31–41. Medford, NJ: Information Today.

This chapter provides an excellent introduction to the argument for redesigning and reimagining the library system, with key needs clearly articulated. It includes Blyberg's ILS Customer Bill of Rights.

Breeding, Marshall. 2012. "Open Software for Libraries: Current Trends and Issues." www.librarytechnology.org/ltg-displaytext.pl?RC=16696.

This webpage links to a PowerPoint presentation, which contains a review of the current implementation of open-source options among libraries, including library systems and discovery layer products, with excellent attention paid to the risks and reward of these packages for libraries.

Brubaker, Noah, Susan Leach-Murray, and Sherri Parker. 2012. "Implementing a Discovery Layer: A Rookie's Season." *Computers in Libraries* 32, no. 3: 12–19.

This article is a case study of the implementation of a discovery layer, drawing on a library consortium's experience in evaluating multiple discovery layer products.

Cibbarelli, Pamela R. 2010. "Helping You Buy ILS." *Computers in Libraries* 30, no. 1: 20–26. www.infotoday.com/cilmag/CILMag_ILSGuide.pdf. Cibbarelli gives a review of the features available in most integrated library systems as well as suggestions on crucial questions for librarians to consider when purchasing a system. The article includes a guide to current ILS vendors and their products.

Free/Open Source Software for Libraries. http://foss4lib.org. This website and electronic discussion list shares libraries' experiences with open-source products and links to available software.

Kuali Open Library Environment (OLE). www.kuali.org/ole. A project funded by the Andrew W. Mellon Foundation to investigate methods and approaches to redesigning library systems, the plan is to devise an open-source, community-built library system that will allow libraries to integrate new technologies.

Library Technology Guides: Key Resources in the Field of Library Automation. www.librarytechnology.org. This website by Marshall Breeding includes links to library automation vendors, library OPACs, and lists of articles on library automation trends and topics.

NGC4LIB (Next Generation Catalogs for Libraries). http://blog.gmane.org/ gmane.culture.libraries.ngc4lib (subscription information and archives). This discussion group offers an ongoing conversation on the development of new catalogs.

OCLC (Online Computer Library Center). www.oclc.org. This is the main OCLC website, which can give you a fuller background and description of their services.

Waller, Nicole. 2003. *Model RFP for Integrated Library System Products. Library Technology Reports* 39, no. 4. Waller authored all the content of this issue of *Library Technology Reports*. The various articles outline the elements that are required to create an RFP and provide sample RFPs. Waller also discusses questions to ask vendors and other considerations for libraries pursuing library systems and ILS products.

CHAPTER 8
STORAGE DEVICES
IN LIBRARIES

MAGNETIC MEDIA AND
OUR OLD FRIEND PAPER

AS NOTED IN CHAPTER 2, there came a point in history when people needed to find a way to share and safeguard information. The quest began with oral history and memorization and has continued ever since, constantly evolving with new ways to record information. As this chapter illustrates, people are still finding novel ways to contain information and pass it along. They are also creating new types of media, just as words on paper have been followed by sound recordings, film, **hypertext documents**, and so on. We need to understand and be able to use these types of items because libraries, as repositories of information, are bound to attract a wide variety of formats. Aside from accessing them and making them available to our patrons, we need to be able to preserve them (or the information in them) for the future.

PAPER
Despite the development of a long list of formats that follow, paper is still a significant means for sharing written information and still images. Many thousands of books are published each year. An ever-growing number of periodicals are available for subscription, though, to be fair, more and more periodicals are moving to electronic-only distribution or launching as digital publications. Libraries are still buying, shelving, and circulating paper products. Unlike many of the media that follow, the technology of printing on paper has not changed drastically over the past century. The materials for printing have grown cheaper, which has had some negative effects on preservation, but nothing incredibly innovative has happened when we

compare this format to the others. Paper is currently a constant for libraries, and it is too early to suggest that its demise is near. Rather than seeing the success of other media for conveying information as a repudiation of paper, we should look at this expansion as a growing diversity of materials, tangible and intangible, that the library needs to provide to its users.

MICROFORMATS

Microformats are fairly traditional formats for libraries, having existed in some form since the turn of the twentieth century. They consist of rolls or single sheets of photographic film with miniaturized images of pages of text or diagrams—the full content of the publication that was preserved there. The rolls are known as **microfilm** and the sheets are **microfiche**. Microfilm can accommodate between 1,000 and 1,500 pages per 100 foot roll of 32 mm film, which is the standard size used in libraries. Microfiche can hold between 60 and 98 pages per sheet in its standard format; there are versions called ultrafiche that can hold larger numbers of pages. Libraries use microfiche primarily for routine storage of periodicals and special collections of documents, and in the past government documents were often distributed on microfiche. Preservation of periodicals was an early driving force for the creation of microformats, and space preservation has helped prolong it as a medium. Art and medical libraries used microformats for images, and print catalogs were transferred to microfiche in some libraries in the 1980s. Both types of microformats require special reading equipment to view them. There are separate readers available for each format, but many microfilm reader/printer units can also be used to view and print microfiche. Another common feature of these units is the ability to scan images from microfilm and microfiche into digital file formats.

COMPACT DISC TECHNOLOGY

Compact disc (CD) technology, invented in the early 1980s, has been used for two purposes: recording high quality sound (compact discs) and providing a stable source for recording data such as text and still images, with the additional advantage of being searchable (**compact disc read-only memory, or CD-ROM**). Both types are widely available, and each one has overtaken an existing media format: compact discs killed off record albums and dominated **audiocassettes** for recorded music, and CD-ROMs largely took the place of 3.5-inch **floppy disks** for distributing software. Libraries include both types in their collections. CDs are borrowed by music lovers, and CD-ROMs may be available with children's software and various other applications. CD-ROMs, the primary format for the multimedia craze of the early 1990s, have been available in libraries as containers for digital reference sources, including encyclopedias and other tools. They are also included with books as carriers of supplemental material.

The technology consists of round, 5.25-inch discs that are pitted by lasers to retain data. CDs can hold a maximum of 74 minutes of very high quality recorded sound. CD-ROMs can contain up to 600 MB of computer data and are considered to be very stable. Unfortunately, CD-ROMs are not very good carriers for video because **CD-ROM drives** cannot play video quickly enough to sustain a fluid display. CD players and CD-ROM drives have been quite common in society and are also found in libraries. Older desktop computers routinely have drives that can play CD-ROMs; current computers are usually equipped with DVD drives instead. CD-RW (compact disc read/write) drives and blank discs are also widely available for computer users to record their own music or data in CD format. Again, most older desktop computers will routinely have drives that can perform CD-RW functions, and newer desktops will likely have DVD drives to play or record this newer media, as discussed in the next section.

DVD TECHNOLOGY

DVD (which stands for nothing, but you will hear digital versatile disc or digital video disc) technology has been around since the late 1990s. It is very similar to CD technology in the following ways: the DVD disc is the same physical size as a CD, it uses a laser-pitting process to place information on the discs, and it comes in multiple formats. When we look at those formats, though, we can see the differences between DVDs and CDs. Audio DVDs can hold fifty hours of sound, **DVD-ROMs** can hold between 4.7 and 17 GB of data, and DVD videos can hold between two and eight hours of high-quality audio and video. DVDs can be single- or double-sided. DVD is a substantial improvement over CD technology in terms of quantities of data, sound, and video, but it is also a revolution in terms of the speed at which they can be played: up to nine times the speed of CDs. The speed issue, combined with its random access to content and its sturdier composition, is what allowed DVD to emerge as the preeminent video storage format over videocassettes.

DVDs do require a separate drive or player to be used. DVD players are commonly available for use with televisions or stereo systems (or a combination) to play the audio and video formats. DVD drives are commonly included with desktop computers, with a nice feature: they will also play CD-ROMs. DVD provides a media format that has great potential in many areas. Libraries need to accommodate both DVDs in their audiovisual collections and as a storage medium that can be accessed on staff and public computers. DVDs are the video format of choice for many libraries given that most patrons have DVD players at home. Libraries that provide viewing stations must have DVD players as well. New computers will typically have DVD-RW drives installed that allow recording to DVDs. We will need to look ahead to greater use of DVDs for software distribution, multimedia application use, and archival storage.

COMPUTER MEMORY OPTIONS

So many of the methods for storing information covered in this chapter are formats that we find on the library shelves (books, videocassettes, CDs, etc.). With so many electronic library resources today existing on library servers, vendors' websites, or elsewhere on the Internet, we need to discuss magnetic media as a storage method. Where do all of the files that make up a full-text periodical index physically sit? Where do you put thousands of hours of digital videos? Generally, they are placed on server hard drives, which can accommodate multiple terabytes (1 TB = 1,000 GB) of data. This is the same situation for almost every document on the Internet: files are sitting on hard drives and can either be downloaded (transferred directly) to a receiving computer's hard drive or can be backed up to other portable forms of magnetic media.

Magnetic media storage devices work by using electrical impulses to inscribe information in a certain pattern on magnetic material. The material is encased in a container of some kind that can then be accessed by the same device to retrieve the information. We briefly discussed storage device and media options back in Chapter 5. Hard drives, flash drives, and magnetic tape all offer storage possibilities for particular purposes.

Hard drives tend to be used to store operating systems, installed software applications, and working or archived files that will be used on a given computer. Current hard drives can contain several hundred gigabytes of data. They can crash or lose files but tend to be pretty safe for data because they stay in one place and are not removed or touched in any way. They are also very convenient to use, in that it is easy to save files you are working on to them and then retrieve those files at a quick speed.

USB flash drives (also known as pen drives, key drives, or thumb drives) are extremely small hard drives that can be used to move files, software, and even whole operating systems from computer to computer. They fit into a category known as **removable storage**. If an individual is routinely working with large files such as image files, video, or PowerPoint presentations and needs to work on a number of different computers (or even at home and at work), saving to removable storage makes a lot of sense. As well, if you would like to back up a huge number of documents or other data files, removable storage is an easy way to do so. Zip and Jaz disks, which look similar to floppy disks but could store between 100 MB and 2 GB, were a transitional form of removal storage that have now been replaced by flash drives.

More than just a way to move files, the flash drive can be a platform for running an operating system or application on one machine and then moving on to run the same software at additional machines. These devices work by simply being plugged into a USB (universal serial bus) port on a computer. Once the system recognizes the new hardware, the flash drive will then show up as a separate drive letter on the machine, much as a hard drive or DVD drive appears. The drives vary in shape and size a bit, but they are generally about two inches long, have a standard USB plug on one end, and are overall narrow and slim enough to fit into a USB port slot without being in the way of other plugged-in devices. With a maximum capacity of 256 GB, they are a powerful option for mobile storage. A smaller capacity flash drive of 2 GB is a great deal cheaper and takes up much less space than the equivalent storage space in floppy disks (or CDs or DVDs).

Magnetic tape is primarily used as an archival storage medium. Here the magnetic material is not contained in a disc but as a reel that can fast-forward or rewind to locate data, similar to that of an audiocassette. Magnetic tape can store a vast amount of data in a compact form, up to several gigabytes of information. The downside of magnetic tape is that information on the tape is inscribed sequentially, meaning that individual files are more difficult to locate. Individual applications cannot be run from magnetic tapes; rather, program files must be loaded on a hard drive to use the application. This medium is excellent for storing data for future use or for completing large backups.

DIGITAL VIDEO COLLECTIONS

Digital video collections are an attractive option for libraries that wish to provide DVD content to remote users or to share it among members of a library consortium. These collections may be created with locally available content, created by members of the library's community. They can also be formed by gaining vendor permission to digitize purchased physical copies of the vendor's titles (hosting the digital video on local servers). Some media distributors offer streaming video services, with library patrons accessing programs from the company's servers. There are also efforts in place in academic libraries to digitize DVDs and videocassettes from their collections which are needed for course reserve (the digitized materials may be retained for future reserve use). Any digitized or originally digital video can be made available as streaming video (where viewers can watch the video through their Internet connections but do not download a copy) or in downloadable form (if the rights to do so are made available by the video's creator). These options give libraries the opportunity to be flexible in how they make video materials available beyond the standard checking out of packaged video items.

DIGITAL VIDEO RECORDERS

Digital video recorders (DVRs) are very popular as ways to store large amounts of video on a hard drive. They are perhaps best known for consumer use in recording large volumes of preset television programs. A set-top device can be added to a television for direct recording to digital. One great benefit of this method is that programs can be watched in uninterrupted enjoyment with commercials removed. Though this element of DVRs has not yet been put to use in libraries as far as I have learned, another purpose may be in use. Closed-circuit television systems used for library security may record their footage on DVRs rather than VCRs, resulting in easily recording of hours of video without having to change out cassettes. We'll see if other applications develop over time.

MP3 FILES AND PLAYERS

Audio files have been available on computers for quite a long time, and they have become widely available on the web (both legally and illegally). The music industry had been wary for some time of selling individual music tracks online, fearing rampant sharing and copying. While this has occurred at points in the past and continues to occur, the development of stricter controls on file sharing (called digital rights management [DRM]) and a seemingly inevitable shift away from "container" music sales (album, cassette, CD) toward single-track use caused music companies to begin selling (or licensing their recordings for sale by others) online. While audio files can be contained in a variety of file types (.cda for audio CDs, .wma as a Windows media format, etc.), **.mp3**, a format that can be played on many different applications and in various makes of players, is the most common term used to speak about this form of media.

Libraries are not directly involved in the collection of individual .mp3 files for their audio collections yet—at least not in large numbers. However, the growth of available downloadable audio and the use of MP3 players could impact future collections. The **iPod**, available in a range of price points, and many other varieties of MP3 players are owned by millions of people. This audience has been approached by libraries with the innovation of .mp3 versions of books on tape. Services such as Recorded Books and OverDrive offer large collections of popular fiction and nonfiction titles as digital audiobooks. The titles may be downloaded and played on a computer, burned to a CD, or transferred to an MP3 player.

Some libraries have purchased MP3 players to check out to their patrons with a selection of audio titles placed on them. Others are making use of products from companies such as Playaway: prerecorded, deck-of-cards sized players with a single digital audiobook on them. These small units are easy to check out to patrons, and their use removes the danger of lost individual CDs from an audiobook set. Others are equipping their public computers for easy CD burning or file transfer to MP3 devices. It will be interesting to watch these developments and see what other information forms are made attractive for an MP3 audience.

SCANNING TECHNOLOGY

Although they are not media formats but rather methods for converting information into various formats, it is important to mention computer scanners, which have been improving significantly over the past several years. Over time, scanners have also become less expensive. A computer needs only a scanner and scanning software to transfer physical items (such as periodical articles and photographs) into digital form. **Optical character recognition (OCR)** software, coupled with scanners, can also be used to turn typewritten or printed copies of text into word-processing documents that can be manipulated. Scanners differ in terms of their resolution (600 dots per inch [dpi] is a good minimum) and their color capabilities (24 to 30 bits color is acceptable). Higher-end scanners are preferable for image scanning.

Libraries have been using scanners to produce digital versions of archival documents in order to display and archive them. Scanners have also proved popular for adding images or documents to library websites as part of the web design process. Another common task is the creation of electronic reserve collections for academic libraries, wherein periodical articles and other publications are scanned into electronic file formats and made accessible over the web to students. The growing use of scanners by libraries to create digital versions of information will have an impact on the eventual archiving of these materials. This interest is often aimed at preserving rare originals and making them available to the public.

YOU *CAN* TAKE IT WITH YOU

Library patrons expect to be able to take library items home with them, and now many methods are available to do so. As libraries' collections continue to grow in their additions of new media types, the ability to copy, print, e-mail, download, and scan items should be provided. Copying and printing are long-standing services in libraries and can almost be overlooked in a discussion of new technologies. E-mail is an option that many electronic resources include, for example, to allow users to enter an e-mail address to send an article or reference book entry to themselves or others. The ability to save full-text articles to flash drives or other media is also helpful. As mentioned, scanning is less common in libraries but would meet the needs of users who would prefer a document in a digital format.

Copying and printing, though they have been in libraries for many years, are affordable technologies and costs are generally passed along to patrons. Scanning is relatively cheap from an equipment standpoint but could be fee based to offset hardware and training costs. The key here is to consider what users prefer in your environment and then try to make it happen. It is easy for libraries to get stuck in a mode of not allowing a particular service (or not pushing for a vendor to include a service, such as e-mailing articles), only later realizing that there is not much of a barrier to making the service happen.

ARCHIVAL ISSUES

Libraries have an interest in storing information, both in its original format if possible and in another one if needed. There are a variety of considerations to make when considering how to store information for the future. For libraries, it is good to begin with an idea of how long a given format will last. Table 8.1 lists the time period you can expect certain popular formats to last if they are kept under optimum conditions (for more information, see Jones, 1999). These conditions require that documents or items are untouched by human

Table 8.1   Archival longevity of different media

Storage Medium	Lifespan
Microfilm and microfiche	200 to 500 years
Books and paper	100 to 500 years
CDs, DVDs, videodiscs	10 to 100 years
Magnetic media (videocassettes, audiocassettes, floppy disks, flash drives, hard drives, magnetic tapes)	10 to 100 years

hands and remain in a room kept at 50° Fahrenheit and 25 percent relative humidity.

No one expects that most materials will ever be kept in optimum conditions. It is interesting, though, that the newer media formats are not predicted to last for anywhere near as long as the more traditional formats. What do the numbers in Table 8.1 mean? First, they should give libraries hope that some of the formats they have heavily invested in (paper and microformats) will be around for a while. They also make clear the fact that to keep some media long term, a change of container or even a change of formats will be needed at some point down the road. The conversion of images in a book (via a scanner) onto a webpage for display and then onto a CD-ROM for archiving purposes or other use is already being done and will continue. The following issues need to be considered about archiving:

- The hardware and software requirements for viewing or hearing a given format need to be considered before you choose it to archive items. It would be a shame to choose a format if its hardware or software became unavailable over time. This is almost unavoidable, however, and so archival collections often include not only the media but its hardware and software that will be needed in the future.
- As mentioned, some thought needs to be given to the best format to keep or whether a new format should be chosen for a given item. Should you keep the eight-track tape of the Doobie Brothers or switch to a CD? Or should you copy it to a DVD? Or create individual .mp3 files for the tracks? Many media allow for easy transfer to a new format for preservation purposes (e.g., copying the contents of floppy disks to a CD-ROM using a CD-RW drive). Others are more

time-consuming or have copyright implications (e.g., scanning a book page by page).

- Can a highly controlled storage environment for archiving items be provided by a library? This factor can affect what you save and how long you can expect items to remain in good condition.
- Consider maintaining multiple copies of items that should be archived. Place one in storage and circulate or use the other.
- Will materials in electronic format remain in high enough use to even bother changing their storage format as time goes on? This is a question for all materials: are they truly of interest to future generations and therefore worth saving? If they are, you need to be thinking of the best ways to preserve them. This is already an issue for electronic formats, which are much less stable than paper.
- Will your nonelectronic formats continue to be used so heavily that they will not last very long? Sometimes this can be solved by purchasing multiple copies, but this is not a financially sound plan for all items. How far do you let a useful item go in regular use before it is too damaged to preserve in another format?
- And what about electronic formats? Will we be able to save our e-mails, webpages, Word documents, and digital images for the enjoyment and edification of future generations? Plans need to be made to back up, archive, and pass along files as individuals leave positions. Too often hard drives are simply reformatted and erased, thus leaving the historical record blank.

Libraries need to seriously consider their archiving options and think about how important preservation is to their overall missions. With careful planning and continuing developments in archival technology, these decisions should grow easier over time.

DEAD AND DYING TECHNOLOGIES

Just for fun, this section mentions some technologies that are basically dead. New titles are rarely distributed in these formats, and they have been superseded by current technologies. A major factor is the near absence of playback equipment for each format. Looking at this list of technologies should be a sobering moment for those of us for whom these technologies were a standard: vinyl records (LPs and 45s), filmstrips, 16 mm film, eight-track tapes, floppy disks (of any size), Zip disks, audiocassettes, laser **videodiscs**, and

Table 8.2 Storage formats for different types of media

Media	Storage Media
Text and still images	Books, periodicals, microformats, computer file storage
Computer files	CD-ROM, DVD-ROM, hard drives, flash drives
Video	DVD, computer files
Audio	CD, DVD, MP3, and other computer files

videocassettes. Which format will join the list next? My money is on CDs with the explosion of .mp3s. Paper? Definitely not yet—and maybe never. Table 8.2 shows current types of media and the storage formats used to contain them.

QUESTIONS FOR REVIEW

1. What are the benefits and downsides of using microformats to store information?
2. How are CDs and DVDs different? What is the technological feature or issue that makes them substantially different in use?
3. How do flash drives and hard drives differ?
4. Name two implications of choosing archival storage formats for information.
5. Does your library offer scanning, copying, printing, downloading, and e-mailing as options for patrons to take articles and other items home with them?
6. Do you remember using any of the dead or dying technologies? Do you still use any of these technologies?

Selected Sources for Further Information

Conservation OnLine (CoOL): Resources for Conservation Professionals. http://cool.conservation-us.org.

CoOL offers an excellent and ever-growing collection of information on the process of preserving materials in all formats.

Crawford, Walt. 2003. "Losing the Legacy of Drives and Ports." *Online* 27, no. 4: 59–60.

The author discusses the end of floppy disks and parallel ports and the model this provides for switching to new media and keeping older peripherals working on new computers.

Donohue, Nanette. 2008. "Nurturing Your Media." *Library Journal* 133, no. 19: 32–35.

    The article covers the growth of audiovisual formats available to libraries and how to add and weed them.

Estes, Marilyn S. 2011. "'Flash' Back: New Format, Old Issues." *Serials Librarian* 61, no. 2: 267–274.

    This article gives an excellent history and overview of USB flash drives and some of the opportunities and challenges they present in library settings.

Jones, Virginia A. 1999. "How Long Will It Last? The Life Expectancy of Information Media." *Office Systems* 99 (December): 42–47.

    Jones provides great background information on the lasting power of the different types of media.

Malczewski, Ben. 2011. "Still Loading." *Library Journal* 136, no. 19: 22.

    This article is an overview of current methods for delivering video in libraries and the implications of these methods on their future adoption and success.

Wilkins, Jesse. 2005. "Migrating to Better Media." *AIIM E-Doc Magazine* 19, no. 1: 17–18.

    In this article, Wilkins discusses the process of moving archival data among storage media.

CHAPTER 9

LIBRARY DATABASES AND ELECTRONIC RESOURCES

FULL-TEXT PERIODICALS, E-BOOKS, AND E-REFERENCE COLLECTIONS

LIBRARY PERIODICAL DATABASES and other **electronic resources** are heavily used as information sources by library staff and patrons. They are some of the ends accessed by the means covered in Chapter 6: the Internet and local networks, and the network cards, modems, and software needed to connect a computer to them. Electronic resources, present in libraries for more than forty years, have continued to grow in functionality, variety, and complexity, as well as number. These sources have influenced libraries' acquisition of more and more computers to accommodate patron access. This chapter details the types of electronic resources used by libraries and the impact of their use.

AVAILABILITY OF ELECTRONIC RESOURCES

The resources described in this chapter are primarily available via the web, though this was not always the case. Historically, electronic resources were available only through direct modem dial-up. A library would use a computer with a modem to connect to a single database or to an online service that offered several different databases (e.g., Dialog or BRS). In time, versions of the databases became available on CD-ROM (compact disc read-only memory), which helped libraries avoid costly **dial-up connection** fees when they installed the CD-ROM locally.

CD-ROMs

While dial-up users paid an annual fee plus a charge for each minute connected, CD-ROM users would pay a single annual fee that could end up being cheaper than staying connected for many hours over a year. The CD-ROMs could be placed on stand-alone computers or be networked for multiple stations or even multiple libraries. Networking a CD-ROM brought in its own expenses, as libraries would have to pay additional licensing fees to have **multiple-user access** to the resource. Libraries could make a CD-ROM available to a set group of computers (e.g., six networked computers within the library) or to a certain number of concurrent users across a larger network (e.g., the computers on an entire college campus).

CD-ROM-based reference resources have generally left libraries, as CD-ROM networked products moved to web-based versions. With the availability of the Internet as an access mechanism, pay-by-the-minute fees have been transformed into annual subscription costs priced on user head counts (e.g., based on enrollment in academic and school libraries or registered borrowers in public libraries). Libraries now pay to connect an entire library and its computers to handle a certain number of simultaneous users in the library's community who connect via the web. Users no longer need to be connected to a local network to gain access to the resource; as long as they are affiliated with the library or its parent organization, they can use the huge network of the Internet for access. Changes in communications technology have increased the flexibility of using these resources for staff and patrons alike.

Periodical Databases

Periodical indexes like the *Readers' Guide to Periodical Literature* were among the first **electronic reference sources**. It is quick and easy to search for article citations in a database by specific fields or by keywords. Add in abstracts and links to full-text articles and these sources become even more convenient for and valuable to library users. Such "one-stop shopping" for articles is possible from within the library or at home. Some excellent examples of general and subject-specific **periodical databases** are those provided by the EBSCOhost, Gale, and ProQuest families of databases.

The current situation represents a drastic change from the periodical research process of twenty years ago. Then it was a time-consuming process that involved flipping through annual volume after annual volume of a periodical index. When I was in college, I would thumb through printed indexes such as *Readers' Guide* or *Social Sciences Index* to find articles that would work for my topic. Those indexes were arranged in alphabetical order by subject heading, and there were times when it was hard to choose the right heading to use. Once I found potentially useful citations for articles, I had to determine whether the library I used owned the periodicals in which the citations appeared. There was a printed volume that alphabetically listed all of the periodicals and gave their locations in the library. Then I would head to the periodicals area of the collection or up into the stacks (depending on which periodical I was after) and track down the correct issue. In some libraries you had to fill out a request slip for each periodical so that the staff could bring the issue to you; patrons were not allowed to browse the issues themselves. Then I would head over to the photocopying area and start the slow process of copying each article. The situation today is heaven by comparison.

The major difference has been the widespread addition of full-text periodical articles to the databases. Publishers and database vendors have worked out agreements to make many thousands of periodicals available in full text. For instance, through our university and our regional consortium, patrons at my library can access more than 30,000 full-text periodicals. "Electronic journals" in libraries can mean a number of different products:

- Electronic versions of printed periodicals are made available on the web by their publishers on a subscription basis (*Science Magazine* at www.sciencemag.org is one example of this). Libraries gain access to the digital version by subscribing to the print periodical and then linking to the web version in their catalog record for the periodical.
- Individual full-text articles from journals and magazines can be found in periodical databases (as described in the previous section).
- Some journals are published only in digital format on the web and may be free or available via subscription. See the Directory of Open Access Journals at www.doaj.org for a directory of free scientific and scholarly e-journals.
- A number of different publishers' journals may be collected together by a library or by a regional consortium. The articles in the collection may be browsed or searched as a group or can be linked from periodical databases that the library or consortium offers. An example of this can be seen at the OhioLINK Electronic Journal Center (http://journals.ohiolink.edu).

Libraries are dependent on these electronic periodical sources, and their use will only grow as more titles become available. Publishers appear to be more and more willing to make their previously print-only content available online.

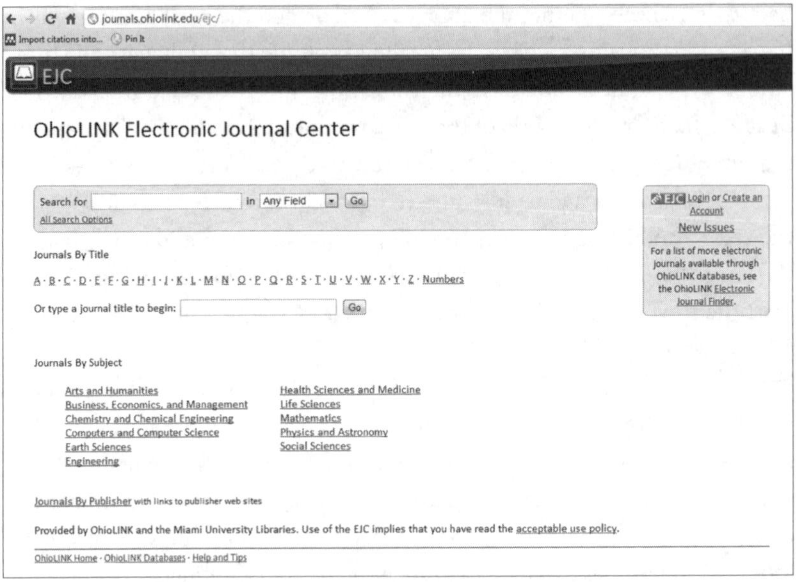

Figure 9.1   Screenshot of OhioLINK Electronic Journal Center

Electronic Books (E-books)

The phenomenon of **electronic books** (**e-books**) brings a new way of experiencing books to the world. Digital versions of books are created (in both text and audio editions) and made available for purchase by libraries and individuals as web-based resources or downloadable files (for reading or listening to at home or elsewhere). While a movement to digitize books that are no longer under copyright protection and post them on the web has been around for years (see Project Gutenberg at www.gutenberg.org), commercial e-books consist of a mixture of newer and older titles. Some companies who distribute them require that you use their specialized software or e-book reader to view them, while other vendors may allow them to work on a variety of e-book readers and other devices. Typically, the software allows you to place bookmarks in an e-book and change text size, among other features. E-book publishers protect their titles through a process known as **digital rights management** (**DRM**), in which various technologies are used to limit copying and printing, thus staying in line with copyright protections on the title. Vendors such as EBSCOhost's eBooks and Audiobooks (www.ebscohost .com/ebooks) and OverDrive (www.overdrive.com) allow you to download text and audio e-books from their collections to various mobile devices or desktop computers. Another alternative for audio e-books is Findaway

World's Playaway digital audio players, in which individuals or libraries purchase a player device that comes preloaded with an individual book title.

It is difficult to tell what this trend means for the traditional book collections of libraries. At this point, many individuals still prefer reading print titles and economic barriers have kept many others from owning e-readers, both of which have likely worked against the widespread adoption of e-books over print. An ever-growing volume of titles, new developments in e-readers like the Barnes and Noble NOOK (www.barnesandnoble.com/NOOK) and the Amazon Kindle (www.amazon.com/kindle), and the introduction of audio e-books have sustained growth and interest in e-books. Though lending of e-readers (with titles chosen by library staff members or choice given to the patron to purchase a title) has begun in earnest, there are no straightforward methods for libraries to buy and lend e-books at will for patrons to use on their own e-readers and mobile devices. Vendors and publishers do make collections of text and audio e-books available for libraries to purchase and then offer for download, but licensing restrictions and expense keep many titles unavailable in e-format. Those with the largest collections of e-books do not make it easy to lend those titles from device to device.

In the academic library world, individual libraries and library consortia have been buying collections of scholarly and reference e-books and making them available to authenticated patrons through the web. Safari Books Online (www.safaribooksonline.com) is an example of a service libraries can use to access multiple publishers' works online, freeing them from buying print copies of technology book titles that become quickly outdated. In addition to these collections, chosen based on topic areas of interest or a highly valued publisher, librarians are now considering how best to choose other e-book titles. One option is called patron-driven authentication (PDA) or demand-driven authentication (DDA). After a librarian preselects a number of e-book titles, links to those books are added into the library's catalog. Then patrons can discover the titles, and if they are used enough (sometimes a rule of ten is used: e.g., ten minutes of use, ten pages viewed, ten individual uses) the library purchases the e-book. It means that a huge number of e-book titles can be made available to a library's patrons, with those patrons having the final say on which titles are purchased.

Electronic Reference Collections

Just as the availability of full-text articles makes research easier, online access to reference sources is a boon to the library's community. Sources include almanacs, dictionaries, directories, encyclopedias, literary criticism collections, and many other selected sources. Most often, they are existing reference sources that are now available digitally. Electronic reference sources today are a bit of a hybrid of periodical databases and e-books. Some were designed as searchable resources specifically for the online environment, and others have moved from print to electronic format while maintaining the ability to browse them page by page in addition to keyword searching.

Libraries are tending toward purchasing only electronic versions of reference sources, buying print versions only when they must. Improved searching is a huge advantage, as is the common ability to have access to regularly updated versions of the sources. These e-sources can also expand on the possibilities of print sources by adding sound (e.g., the ability to listen to Martin Luther King Jr.'s recorded speeches rather than just reading his words) and video (e.g., watching the human immune system attack a virus in a computer model) to help users appreciate and understand the material. Not to be missed from this discussion is the fact that these electronic resources can be used by multiple individuals and, through authentication, from anywhere that users have Internet access, bringing the full-text, image-bearing source into the user's home. The space gained by removing print reference collections can be reallocated to patron space or other uses.

ELECTRONIC ACCESS ISSUES

We will consider a number of advantages and disadvantages of electronic resources later in this chapter. Before that, though, there are a number of issues relating to their access that we must address.

Multiple User Identification

Libraries can provide simultaneous access to electronic resources for multiple users. A variety of issues are of concern when we consider the access we wish our community to have to a resource. Multiple user access tends to be the norm for most resources. We need to consider where we would like to provide access, to whom we would like to provide access, and how we will ensure that only those designated people can access the resource.

Authentication is crucial for remote access because the licensing agreements we sign when we subscribe will specify our responsibility for ensuring that only authenticated users are using the resource. It can be accomplished by having remote users log in on the library's proxy server (providing a username—library card number, student ID, etc.—and a personal identification number or password) before allowing users to use the resource. Authentication can also be done from within the library by providing the vendor with a certain range of IP addresses from which the resource should be available.

Technological Requirements

The other access issue beyond meeting authentication requirements is the technology issue: what technology components do a library or an individual need to access the resource? This can include the speed of an Internet connection, the minimum characteristics for a computer, and perhaps the type and version of web browser software. We need to be aware of the minimum requirements for a resource both for equipping our in-house computers and for deciding whether enough of our patron base can use the resource remotely. The technology requirements must be available to users so that they can determine whether they will be able to successfully use the resource remotely. Additionally, a library needs to make enough computers available to accommodate users. For staff-oriented resources, budgeting to upgrade staff computers will be needed if the current resources do not meet minimum requirements.

Cost

Cost is noted as a potential disadvantage of electronic resources. In some cases, electronic resources can be bargains for a library when compared to purchasing the equivalent print resource. This can stand out in the case of full-text periodical resources where you might cancel a print subscription as well as the microfilm for a title, realizing substantial savings. On the other hand, some electronic resource agreements will require that you maintain your print subscription to the same source for a certain amount of time, thus forcing you to pay twice for the same product. Careful consideration needs to be made regarding whether an electronic resource will be a feasible expense. Beyond the subscription cost, libraries need to consider the staff time involved in updating software or loading updates to the database itself. In the case of databases that are maintained on a library's own server, the maintenance of the database files and their updates can differ in the time required from resource to resource.

In the case of separate subscriptions to full-text periodicals or electronic journals, libraries face a situation not much different from the one they see with print serial collections. Costs for serials rise dramatically each year, and libraries may find themselves unable to continue with certain electronic subscriptions. The most striking situation has been among scholarly publications and some large publishers such as Elsevier. A number of academic library consortia have had to threaten (and some to fulfill their threats) to cancel their subscriptions from a given publisher to head off substantial price increases from year to year. There is also an "open access" movement afoot in academic circles to make research articles available online at no charge to the scholarly community, thus bypassing the expensive subscription prices that libraries and others must pay for scientific publications. A loose coalition of scholarly associations, libraries, and publishers is working to improve this situation for everyone involved.

Canceling Print Sources

When we have, either by design or happenstance, duplicated one of our print sources with electronic ones (reference books or periodicals), it will probably occur to someone that we should cancel the print version. This happens quite frequently with periodical databases or with **source aggregators** like LexisNexis, which includes a variety of full-text periodicals and reference sources in its databases. This can certainly save us money. The potential downside is that if a particular title is ever removed from the database, we may end up with a gap in our collection. In libraries where the current version of a source is used to the exclusion of any earlier ones, the impact of this loss may be small. However, in other situations, missing a year or two of a heavily utilized periodical title can be disastrous and confusing to patrons—some of whom will inevitably need *only* the year we happen to be missing from our collection. We need to remember that our subscription to an electronic resource does not guarantee that it will remain the same over the course of the subscription; and to be fair, many resources improve their electronic versions over time. The great gain of wider access (beyond the library) is generally worth this potential unpredictability.

Organizing and Integrating

Libraries have long been focused on bringing disparate resources together and organizing them so that they can be found and used. The question libraries face now is: how can we put electronic and print sources together so that they can be used effectively without one type or another getting lost? On the staff side, library staff must understand where and when to use print resources and where and when to use electronic ones. The issues on the public side of electronic resources are much the same. When we arrange electronic resources on our library websites, how can we be sure to lead our patrons to print sources when they are the best ones to use? **Online pathfinders** for a given topic that list electronic and print sources side by side can help. For example, see Miami University Libraries' Research by Subject (http://libguides.lib.muohio.edu), as shown in Figure 9.2, or Kansas City Public Library's Resources by Topic (www.kclibrary.org/resources-by-topic/). Another alternative for libraries is LibGuides (www.springshare.com/libguides/), a subscription-based service that provides for easy creation of subject-related guides. Library staff must also be educated to lead patrons to the most appropriate source, not just the easiest one to find on the shelf or website.

A related integration issue is that of connecting potentially several sources or collections of full-text periodicals and the library's print or microfilm periodicals with periodical indexes. Library users can expect that most periodical databases will have their own selections of full-text coverage. A method for connecting each individual database's **full text**, so that a search in Periodical Index A will show links to full-text articles from Periodical Index B,

Figure 9.2   Screenshot of Miami University Libraries' Research by Subject page

Electronic Journal Collection X, *and* Periodical Index A, is called OpenURL (briefly mentioned in Chapter 7). **OpenURL** is a protocol for making connections between the indexing databases and the full-text sources through an OpenURL server that includes a database showing periodical title coverages and interlinkages. An excellent example of this in action is OhioLINK's OLinks service (http://olinks.ohiolink.edu).

Federated Search and Discovery Layers

"Why can't we just search all of these tools at once?" This question has occurred to many a library staff member and library user confronted with a sometimes overwhelming number of electronic resources. Given that the electronic resources described here, irrespective of type, are all available electronically and are all able to be searched by keyword, it is possible to pursue **federated search**: searching multiple sources from a single search blank. Federated searching is also known as metasearch. The existence of Internet search engines that allowed for metasearch of multiple search engines at once, such as Dogpile (www.dogpile.com), was also a motivating factor for developing metasearch in library resources. Between systems created in house by library systems staff and commercial products, federated searching has been implemented in hundreds of libraries. Now the move is toward a discovery layer, as described in Chapter 7.

The concept is fairly straightforward: a library can have a search blank on its website for users to simultaneously search the OPAC, a number of periodical databases, locally held collections of electronic resources, e-books, and the web. The result is a relevance-ranked mixture of sources that matches the terms you entered. The "discovery" element is that many resources unknown to patrons (e.g., e-books or scholarly articles) become part of the results, having been discovered by the software. The most fitting set of articles, books, websites, and e-reference source materials available are, in theory, presented for your topic. You are then able to scan down the list of results without worrying about where the items have come from.

This result was sought with federated searching, with sometimes mixed results: sources were not necessarily searched with meaningful relevancy ranking applied to the results, or duplicate sources from multiple databases were not removed. A large result set could be produced that proved confusing to users. With discovery layers, the available databases and individual sources are supposedly much better indexed and relevance is assessed more carefully. There is also the ability to shape the initial and succeeding result sets through the use of multiple facets (type of publication, format of item, date, availability, etc.). The guidance provided through the interface can help you shape the search. Libraries cannot count on even the best software to control the relevance of results for very broad searches, such as "war" or "America." It is certainly true that users are probably better off learning about specific tools so that they can selectively choose the best resources. However, this is very much a librarian way of thinking; we cannot expect our users to have or take the time to learn everything that we know. There are research needs for which a one-stop search option would save the time of the user and reveal incredibly useful sources. An alphabetical list of 100 or 200 databases can be difficult to dive into. Tying together many, if not all, of the resources in our collections presents users with a fuller picture of what a library has available for them.

Training and Education

Training is crucial to the successful use of electronic resources in a library. If patrons do not understand how (or when) to use the resources, and if staff are also ignorant in this way, the library will have wasted a lot of money and not served its patrons. Any implementation of electronic information sources needs to be accompanied by intensive staff training. Part of this training needs to be aimed at how staff members can help educate patrons who have questions about the new resources or are encountering them for the first time. This should be done in addition to any formal public instruction program the library may have. Using **screencasts** is an effective means for providing quick training that is easy to review (and great for visual learners). One useful set of these brief video tutorials may be found at the ANTS (Animated Tutorial Sharing Project) collection on Screencast.com (www.screencast.com/users/ANTS). Chapter 14 offers a variety of other methods aimed at instructing users. Remember that resources can be used effectively and live up to their potential only if those who use them know what they are doing.

ADVANTAGES AND DISADVANTAGES OF ELECTRONIC LIBRARY RESOURCES

We have already looked in this chapter at some positive reasons for utilizing electronic information sources. In this section we review advantages and disadvantages of these resources and their use, not all of which apply to each category of resource. These lists will provide you with background information that will help in the next section's discussion of some overall issues raised by these resources.

Advantages
- Electronic resources are easier to search because they offer more varied search options than do print-based resources.
- Related to the first point, electronic resources are located on the web and use interfaces similar to other search engines with which users may already be familiar. People are used to turning to the web as a central location for information-seeking activities, so why not place library resources in easy proximity?
- Electronic resources provide services that are not duplicated in other formats, such as the integration of full-text articles within periodical indexes.
- The resources are more accessible than print resources; they can be used by multiple users at the same time and can be made available remotely to the library's community.
- Using electronic resources can save space in libraries, for example, using full-text online periodicals rather than microfilm or bound periodicals, or using electronic reference sources in place of reference books.
- These resources are cheaper to access in the long run and are easier to update; current data can be added to one central site that is available to all users of the resource.

Disadvantages
- Electronic resources can be prohibitively expensive for some libraries; at the very least, they require libraries to carefully examine what they will be getting before they subscribe.
- The resources can stop working at inopportune times due to local networking failures or due to difficulties at the server site.
- They can be difficult to browse through for some topics, as keyword searching brings up only exact matches, which may be less helpful than thumbing through a periodical index or reference book.
- Electronic resources may not be exact replicas of existing print versions or may lose information sources over time—especially in the case of full-text periodical resources, which may lose the rights to provide certain periodicals.

In general, electronic library resources force a library to ask some hard questions about its provision of services. When we move from print to online resources, we need to know what we will do when the resource is not available: what is our backup plan? We need to consider how providing full-text resources will change what is printed in the library and how many reams of paper we will start using in a month—or a day. The good thing is that electronic library resources can expand the choices our patrons have. The difficult element is that as we add these resources we grow more and more dependent on resources over which we have little control and barely any ownership. The reality is that electronic resources are an inevitable addition for any library, and the best bet is to pursue cooperative licensing arrangements and possibly purchase digital content with other libraries. This is the present and future of libraries.

QUESTIONS FOR REVIEW

1. Describe the different ways that a library might have access to full-text periodical articles.
2. What are two advantages and two disadvantages of electronic resources?
3. What is a key difference in today's use of electronic resources when compared to the early days of these resources?
4. Explain discovery layers. Does your library offer this service?
5. Do you feel adequately trained in the use of electronic resources in your library? Who in your library or elsewhere could help you learn more (remember the resources in Chapter 3)?

Selected Sources for Further Information

CUFTS Maintenance Tool: Compare Resources. http://cufts2.lib.sfu.ca/MaintTool/public/compare.

This resource from the Simon Fraser University Library provides libraries with the ability to compare two to four periodical databases with one another for overall coverage and full-text access to periodical titles.

Hoeppner, Athena. 2012. "The Ins and Outs of Evaluating Web-Scale Discovery Services." *Computers in Libraries* 32, no. 3: 6–40.

An excellent background to the workings of discovery systems and how they work, along with a comparison of four discovery layer products.

Polanka, Sue, ed. 2012. *No Shelf Required 2: Use and Management of Electronic Books*. Chicago: American Library Association.

Polanka had edited an excellent collection of chapters by twenty contributors on aspects of implementing e-books in various library settings.

Weir, Ryan. 2012. *Managing Electronic Resources: A LITA Guide*. Chicago: ALA TechSource.

This is a practical guide to the many issues involved in choosing the implementing electronic resources in the library. It also offers tips on organizing and accessing digital content.

CHAPTER 10

THE INTERNET'S IMPACT ON FINDING INFORMATION

A IS FOR AMAZON, *G* IS FOR GOOGLE

THE INTERNET IS AN exciting venue for information seeking and sharing. It is important for library staff to understand not only the Internet technology that connects them and their patrons to library-licensed resources but also the complexity of online information and how to find it. Library staff members have moved away from the dark days of reacting to online information with distrust. Critical thinking and information evaluation skills are a must for us and our patrons. We cannot forget, though, that our library databases and catalogs are competing for attention with Internet information providers who have created compelling and popular methods for connecting people with information. This chapter explores the Internet from a user's and a library's perspective, discusses searching the Internet for information, and addresses how libraries should consider taking their time-tested information sources back to the drawing board.

THE INTERNET

The Internet is a global computer network that has revolutionized communications and information exchange. As the Internet has grown in commercial and social applications, it is essential for libraries to provide access to it and to use it themselves for information gathering and provision.

The origins of the Internet go back to the 1950s and 1960s when teams at chosen universities in the United States, involving government research-ers and sponsored by government defense groups, began trying to develop computer communication networks. In 1969, after years of work, ARPANET (Advanced Research Projects Agency Network) successfully transmitted the first snippets of information on its new and fragile network, which would eventually become the precursor to the Internet that we know today. By 1969, when the pre-Internet was born, it was hoped that it would become a way to securely share information among researchers working on military research projects in geographically disparate locations. The U.S. military also wanted the network to continue to operate even if some of the connected computers were, say, destroyed in a nuclear attack. The result was a worldwide collection of host computers using high-speed telephone lines to share information. The military research focus slowly gave way to more general uses by academic researchers. As the number of educational and then business users grew, the Internet erupted as a public utility in the early 1990s. Individuals with no ties to education, business, or the military were able to get online, which vastly increased the number of Internet users. The U.S. government turned over its operation of the host computers that routed Internet communications, the Internet "backbone," to private telecommunications companies. The Internet continued to grow.

We now find the Internet as a huge collection of computers and information that is experienced daily by hundreds of millions of people. It is a mixture of relevant and irrelevant services and information, and it is available to a huge percentage of the population—yet is unavailable to society's poorest members except through public institutions like libraries. There is serious money at work in the Internet, as companies and organizations establish a presence for their services and search for ways to sell services online. It is also a haven for less financially rewarding but no less valuable activities, such as recreational chatting, updating friends, sharing support for those in crisis, and exchanging professional advice. There is a freedom to the Internet: the freedom to communicate, to search out information, and to share. As one might expect, there are sometimes conflicts when this sharing happens, as in the case of recording companies and musicians suing individuals who freely share copyrighted audio files of songs online.

What is the Internet? It is in many ways a reflection and an extension of the rest of the world, and as such it is valuable to libraries and individuals seeking information about that world.

WHAT CAN YOU DO ON THE INTERNET?

The answer to this question grows longer each year as new services and content become available. There are, however, three main things we can do on the Internet: communicate, locate information, and share files.

An important computing concept that propels these uses of the Internet is a process known as **client/server**, in which a piece of software on your computer (the client) can be used to communicate with one or more databases (the servers) to retrieve information or complete an activity. When you use the Internet, you are running a client application on your computer (an e-mail program, a web browser, chat software, etc.) to connect to the servers online.

Communication

There are a variety of ways to communicate on the Internet. It is an exciting prospect: the ability to exchange thoughts, requests, and answers with people located all over the planet. E-mail is the most common method of online communication and the one with roots back to the Internet's beginnings. It allows users to type and send messages back and forth. Messages can be sent to a single individual or to a group of Internet users via an electronic discussion group. Some common e-mail clients are Microsoft Outlook and Mail. People also use **webmail** options (e.g., Gmail, Yahoo! Mail, and Windows Live Mail) where no local software is required, other than a web browser.

Chat and instant messaging are more interactive means of communication where users type brief messages to one another in real time. **Chat** tends to be a web-based technology in which users gather electronically at a set location and communicate on a given topic or whatever is on their minds. **Instant messaging (IM)** is conducted on a one-to-one basis through freely available IM clients communicating through a central server. Similar modes of communication (in content though not technology) include **Usenet** newsgroups and web **bulletin boards**. These tools tend to resemble e-mail in that they allow interested parties to exchange static messages. Their difference from IM and chat is that the messages remain available to the general public on websites.

Not be left out of this discussion are blogs and wikis. **Blogs** (or **web logs**) are online diaries or journals in which an individual or a group can post entries about topics of interest. Entries (or posts) are arranged in reverse chronological order (with the most recent posts appearing first). Readers of the blog can often make comments on the posts to continue the discussion. **Wikis** are websites that can be edited, updated, and improved by anyone who is invited to do so (some, like Wikipedia, are open to the general public for editing). They are used for group work on documents or shared projects and also for larger communities who congregate online to share information through the wikis. These are very interesting developments in information sharing that are having a strong impact on how news spreads and people work together online.

Locating Information

Information sharing is done actively through the communication methods mentioned. Passive display of information online is primarily through the web. Internet users can use **browser software** to visit the millions of documents available on websites. Google Chrome, Microsoft Internet Explorer, Mozilla Firefox, and Opera are four common varieties of browser software. Each website has a **URL** (or **Uniform Resource Locator**; for example, www.neal -schuman.com) that a user can enter into the browser to connect to the site. The sites are created using **hypertext markup language** (**HTML**), a versatile and relatively easy tool that helps create pages of information on the web. Anyone can place information on the web, and there is a great mixture of organizational and personal information available. Though the web can be characterized as passive, it does more than exhibit static text documents; online you will find images of all kinds, audio and video clips, interactive tutorials, games, and much more. Add-on software programs (e.g., media players for sound and video, VOIP [voice-over Internet protocol] applications, and others) are often available for free download.

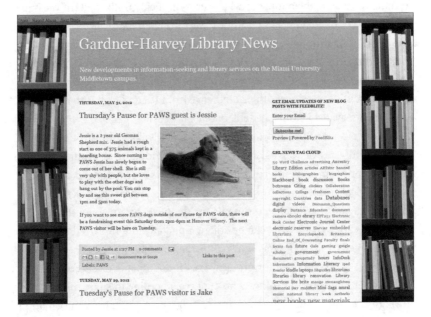

Figure 10.1   Screenshot of a blog

It should be noted that locating Internet information is typified more by searching than browsing. The interlinking of web information through **hyperlinks** does allow some movement from site to site, but more often than not users will examine sites that they find through search tools. Dating back to the early 1990s there have been search devices that allowed a user to enter keywords to locate Internet sites. These tools are often broken into two categories: **search engines**, which allow for keyword searches of large (many billions of pages) segments of the Internet, and search directories, which are human-gathered and human-organized collections of sites that may be searched or browsed. A good example of the former is Google (www.google .com); one of the latter is ipl2 (www.ipl.org).

Sharing Files

While e-mail and the web get the most attention from Internet users, the ability to share files is a crucial aspect of the Internet. Individuals can send word-processing documents or image files back and forth for collaborative purposes. Software companies can place demonstration versions of their products on a website and allow people to download them to their computers to try them out. Despite the dangers posed by computer **viruses** potentially contained in files, many software solutions and safe collections of files are available. While a lot of information on the Internet is available in online discussions or on webpages, it is easy to overlook the mountains of facts contained in files of various formats.

WHY DO LIBRARIES USE THE INTERNET?

Libraries have come to rely on the Internet just as other organizations have. Despite some apprehension on the part of librarians who were not comfortable with computer technology or who wondered whether the Internet would replace libraries, the Internet is well suited to aid and reinforce many of their activities and services. There are five basic ways that libraries use the Internet:

1. *Libraries use the Internet to market themselves and to provide their services.* The primary way that libraries do this is through a library website (more on this in Chapter 13). Libraries place information about their services, contact information, and organized lists of resource links on their sites. Since the web is used so heavily as a marketing tool by the rest of the world, it is sensible for libraries to also take advantage. In addition, libraries provide actual services over the Internet. Reference

service is offered to patrons using e-mail and web-based forms, and requests to purchase materials or for librarians to conduct instruction sessions can be received the same way.

2. *Library staff members use the Internet to communicate with one another, with colleagues, and with patrons.* Staff can consult with colleagues in other libraries about equipment needs, service policies, and reference strategies, among other needs. E-mail gives staff another way to make contact and pass information along to fellow staff members. Staff also receive e-mails from members of their communities. IM is growing in use as a staff communication tool and as a way to provide additional reference assistance to patrons.

3. *Library staff and users search the Internet for information.* Depending on the question, staff can turn to the Internet as a first, last, or middle source in their search strategies for reference questions. Library users are already using the Internet as a source for locating information, often in preference to libraries. Libraries need to help guide users to the best information sources for their need. We also need to accept that sometimes the Internet is the best source and make sure that we can guide people in its use.

4. *Libraries use the Internet as a platform for providing access to resources.* A website is the most logical way for libraries to offer access to their resources because both subscription-based and free electronic resources are typically accessible only on the web. Libraries' websites give patrons a useful, organized listing of electronic resources, or so we hope. As Chapter 9 detailed, some libraries will incorporate print resources (and their call numbers) into websites along with the electronic sources to further integrate their reference collections.

5. *Library staff members use the Internet to research service methods and product information.* Many resources on the Internet can be helpful for finding information in these areas. As mentioned, library staff can turn to colleagues for advice on methods and practices. Discussion groups exist for every type of library and specialty within libraries. The sources listed in Chapter 3 are evidence for the case of product information. In addition, most library vendors have websites to use for surveying their products and contacting them.

INTERNET ISSUES IN LIBRARIES

Nothing in this world is without problems. The Internet has brought a lot of good into the work of libraries and the research of our patrons, but we cannot overlook some problems. The first issue is one alluded to previously: some patrons are dependent on the Internet for information, often to the point of ignoring libraries. This problem has two aspects: first, our patrons—especially those who already ignore the library—need to be educated on the merits of particular library resources for meeting their needs; second, we as library staff cannot fall into the trap of beating down the Internet to raise ourselves up. The Internet needs to be treated by everyone as just another information resource, better in meeting some research needs and worse in others.

The next issue also involves patrons having too much of a focus on the Internet when they are in our libraries. This time it involves viewing materials within the library that is offensive to others—particularly pornography. Some might add to this behavior the tendency of patrons to use library computers to IM, use personal e-mail or Facebook, or play web-based games. Both activities can be offensive to staff and other patrons: the first to staff and patrons who do not wish to view the objectionable material; the second to patrons who have to wait to use a computer—which is also frustrating for staff. Technological solutions for both cases have involved software that attempts to eliminate access to potentially offensive websites or programs that block access to some services like chat and e-mail.

Some libraries have chosen to install—and others have resisted installing—**filtering software**: applications that attempt to restrict access to offensive sites. The software does not necessarily work as it should and can block sites without any offensive content. However, without some steps taken, ranging from user education to filtering, children and others in libraries are able to find or are forced to see images they would rather avoid. The American Library Association opposes mandatory filtering on First Amendment grounds. (See ALA's Filters and Filtering webpage at www.ala.org/ala/issues advocacy/intfreedom/filtering.) There is no easy answer to this situation, and neither unadulterated access nor filtering is without its casualties. It is an issue that libraries will continue to face for some time.

LESSONS FROM THE INTERNET FOR LIBRARIES

As this chapter has thus far demonstrated, the Internet is widely used by society and library staff alike. While it sometimes appears that people are merely running from site to site on the Internet as though following fads, there is something compelling about certain sites that build repeat business. Whether or not people would identify themselves in this way, they are exhibiting a certain amount of brand loyalty to individual sites—and to other sites that copy their approaches. What can libraries learn from this combination of societal trends, interactivity, web design, and new approaches to building community? Is any of this applicable to the library environment? Three case studies follow for consideration.

Amazon.com

Amazon (www.amazon.com) has built a successful business selling books, DVDs, e-books, e-book readers, tablets, and myriad other products through its website. This site provides a useful resource for library staff in locating items, confirming their publication information, and ordering them for library collections. Beyond this impact on libraries, though, elements of the Amazon.com website make it a first choice for people rather than turning to their local library catalog. First, though, let me remove two issues: (1) that individuals may wish to buy books rather than borrow them and (2) that Amazon's catalog is bound to have many more items than that of an individual library. Following are four interesting aspects of the website that may cause people to turn to Amazon first:

- Amazon displays selected pages from many books in its catalog so that users can sample the item before purchasing it.
- The full text of a growing number of items can be searched, along with citation information for all other items, from the search blank on every Amazon page.
- Customers can read and write reviews of Amazon items, assisting them in choosing books and encouraging them to express their own opinions.
- Amazon suggests additional items that might be related to the item in question (the familiar "Customers who viewed this item also viewed . . ."). These suggestions allow users to consider items that did not appear in their original search.

Google

Google (www.google.com) has emerged as the predominant Internet search engine and has held its lead over a variety of competitors. In an industry where, for many years, the race to the biggest database of pages to search drove the competition (and created a new king every six months to a year), Google has held its own on size but added other dimensions:

- The simple, single-lined search blank of Google is a wonderful example of a simple design. There is nothing unclear about their homepage, and there are no decisions to make: just type your search and get results.

- The results screen is very straightforward as well: a list of sites that match the terms entered, ranked by relevance, presented with a selection of the matching text on the page and its URL. Just scan down to choose a link that might meet your need.
- The "Similar" hotlink that appears when you preview a link in the results gives users the opportunity to see if a useful site might lead them to others in the Google database.
- The profusion of specialized searching functions within Google keeps users returning. From Google Maps (maps and directions) and Shopping (a price comparison search) to Images, News, and Scholar (an index of online scholarly articles), Google conveys the impression to users that not much escapes its knowledge. With the advent of the Google Books scanning project, and provision of many of these titles on the web, not much may.

Folksonomies and Social Bookmarking

There are a variety of tools on the Internet now that allow users to collect and share lists of items: website links such as Diigo (www.diigo.com) and Reddit (www.reddit.com), video sites such as YouTube (www.youtube.com), and image-sharing sites like Flickr (www.flickr.com). Communities of users can form around common interests, leading to a great deal of (at least online) social interaction and sharing of information. In addition to making these items visible to other users of the services, and being able to see how many other users linked the same item, a user can classify each link, creating a folksonomy. A **folksonomy** is a "socially constructed classification system" (Smith, 2004). The idea is that instead of using a set classification system (like the Library of Congress Subject Headings [LCSH], for example), the user decides how to describe the item. These sites yield the following interesting aspects:

- They create lists of interesting sources and share them with others.
- They provide the ability for one user to see what others have linked to, gauging the popularity of specific items and following a trail of related items.
- They allow users to assign self-chosen descriptive terms to items, creating a workable vocabulary for organizing items and contributing to a community's choices for terms.

- They give the users of the sites the ability to see the relative popularity of given terms and topics in the larger collection of items.

Library catalogs and websites do not do the things listed in these cases. Could they? Should they? What about other library resources? Should individual periodical articles have "Patrons who viewed this article also viewed . . ." links on their citation screens? The following list suggests what we can learn from these examples and how our library resources may well evolve.

- People are social by nature, and libraries could do much to allow for interaction and sharing of interests within our resources. Could we let patrons write reviews of items in the catalog? What about sharing lists of books, DVDs, and articles that they liked? There are privacy concerns here, by all means, but there could be a path that would be acceptable to consenting patrons.
- The ability to let users choose terms that people actually use to describe items in addition to using standard classification systems

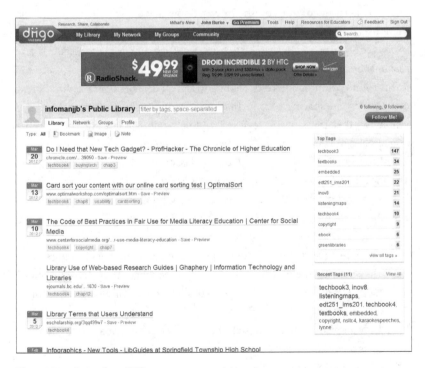

Figure 10.2   Screenshot of Diigo

would be a very interesting development. Libraries may not be ready to let the inmates run the asylum, but we have to face the fact that people do not think in LCSH. That is part of the success of Google as well as folksonomies.

- Can we cut down on some of the options on our pages and help users make a beeline to searching our collections? Google's example might suggest that we can, and the discussion of discovery layers in Chapter 9 suggests that the technology is there to integrate multiple types of sources into a searchable index. The question here is whether library staff members are dismissing the "Googlization" approach because it makes them uncomfortable or they truly believe patrons are short-changed by it.

- Are there ways to make connections between individual information sources that are not dependent on LCSH or even highly relevant key-words? Libraries need to see and understand the success of interlinking in social bookmarking tools and on Amazon as a model for us to institute in our services.

QUESTIONS FOR REVIEW

1. What are three main activities individuals can pursue using the Internet?
2. Name some common library uses for the Internet.
3. Does your library have filtering software installed? Why or why not?
4. What is your reaction to the idea of adding approaches from folksonomies, Google, and Amazon to library resources?
5. Explain the difference between search engines and search directories.

Selected Sources for Further Information

Crosby, Connie. 2010. *Effective Blogging for Libraries*. New York: Neal-Schuman.

Crosby provides an explanation of the process of blogging and suggests ways for libraries to use blogs for marketing and promotional purposes.

Dempsey, Lorcan. 2005. "The User Interface That Isn't." *Lorcan Dempsey's Weblog: On Libraries, Services, and Networks*, May 15. http://orweblog .oclc.org/archives/000667.html.

This post discusses the possibilities of making library interfaces more like those of Amazon and Google. Dempsey suggests there would be benefits for doing so.

Fay, Robin M., and Michael P. Sauers. 2012. *Semantic Web Technologies and Social Searching for Librarians*. Chicago: ALA TechSource.

This book reviews current search tools and how they operate, with the aim of teaching librarians how to strategically search the web and to make their libraries' content findable. It provides a helpful introduction to a variety of tools.

Randeree, Ebrahim, and Lorri Mon. 2011. "Searching for Answers in a Google World." *Reference Librarian* 52, no. 4: 342–351.

This article is an exploration of how to connect with students who rely on Google and show them the value of library resources and approaches to information seeking; it also covers innovations used by Google and Amazon.

Search Engine Showdown: The Users' Guide to Web Searching. http://search engineshowdown.com.

This site has reviews of web search tools and investigations of how they operate.

Yoose, Becky. 2011. "Wiki Adoption and Use in Academic Library Technical Services: An Exploratory Study." *Technical Services Quarterly* 28, no. 2: 132–159.

This article provides an overview of wikis and illustrates a variety of ways they are used within library organizations, with special emphasis on their use in technical services.

CHAPTER 11
WEB 2.0 AND LIBRARIES

FACEBOOK, TWITTER, YOUTUBE, AND SKYPE

IN CHAPTER TEN WE discussed the general outlines of technologies and services available on the Internet. Left out of the discussion until now are some additional technologies that are crucial to how the web operates today and how library staff members can reach out and interact with patrons. They all, it could be argued, represent means of communication between individuals and groups of people. These tools are new forums for interaction, collaboration, and creativity. Larger than that, though, they also allow for new ways to share content online and re-create content to more user-specific needs. All of these concepts are grouped into the term *Web 2.0*, which describes the more participatory, social elements of the web itself. This chapter takes a tour of these technologies and how our patrons are already using them. Now it is time for library staff members to decide how to best implement them.

SOCIAL NETWORKING TOOLS
Social networks are a natural formation of bonds among individuals based on geography, careers, or interests. Social networking applications have arisen as a way for people to bond online and chat, exchange pictures and videos, and stay connected through a medium they use daily. People join the networks, post as much or as little personal information as they would like, connect with people they already know in daily life, add on new "virtual" friends drawn from shared interests, or locate and reconnect with old friends who are geographically distant. You can send out "friend requests" to invite someone to share access to your individual profile pages. Two examples of social networks are Facebook (www.facebook.com) and Google+ (http://plus .google.com).

Figure 11.1   Screenshot of Facebook

Many libraries, along with other organizations, have created presences in social networks. The huge popularity of the networks has made this a natural draw. In some cases this has been effective, but in others there have been few interested parties who wish to "friend" the library. An alternative arrangement has been for library staff members to personally join the network, creating real relationships they can build in both the virtual and three-dimensional worlds. Apart from the overall goal of going where our patrons are, there is the ability to regularly and easily update your entire group of friends (e.g., with announcements about new programs or databases at the library) and to post links to helpful resources and timely information about the library. There is a balance between just being present in a social networking site and actively sharing in that site, which some library patrons may find intrusive—and oth-

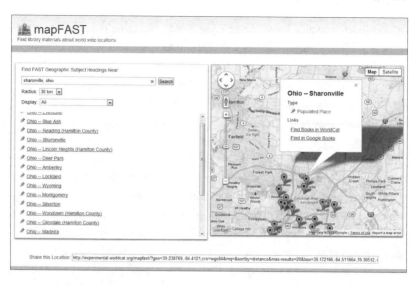

Figure 11.2   Screenshot of mapFAST

ers will really appreciate. This is an ever-evolving situation that you'll need to judge for each library setting.

MASHUPS

A **mashup** is a combination of multiple data sources to serve a combined purpose. One example is to take a web service like Google Maps (http://maps .google.com) and connect its geographic information to something else. For instance, OCLC (Online Computer Library Center) has combined the geographical information on items in WorldCat with Google Maps so that you can search for a location, see it on a map, and then click on that map location to see items about that location in WorldCat or Google Books. It is called mapFAST (http://experimental.worldcat.org/mapfast). There are many possibilities here to use maps for library promotion. A blog that tracks similar uses of Google Maps can be found at http://googlemapsmania.blogspot.com.

LibraryThing (www.librarything.com) is an example of a mashup writ fairly large. It is a community of readers who are able to create personal libraries of books they own or have read. The ability of these readers to discuss books with one another and to tag the items they add puts the service well into the Web 2.0 category. The mashup side of LibraryThing is one of its strengths: users can draw in specific information about each book from the Library of Congress or Amazon (two large repositories for bibliographic information) and also locate cover images of books to help display their collections. LibraryThing combines the personal selections of one individual with the commentary and subject **tagging** of many other individuals and the bibliographic data of other providers. The overall impact is a powerful representation of a work from its physical description to specific commentary on it from the user who added it to its place in the larger pantheon of works added by LibraryThing members.

LibraryThing is extremely attractive to the computer literate bibliophile but has relevance for library staff members as well. While anyone can create a free catalog of their items on the site, libraries may be interested in bringing elements of LibraryThing into their own catalogs (e.g., the tags on a given item and its image may be added to the library's catalog for a fee paid to LibraryThing). The representation of book information in the site has been inspirational to those planning new interfaces. Could we all just catalog our items in LibraryThing? Well, maybe. It does provide a model of a finding tool that has great user involvement.

Yet another mashup is a customized search engine (CSE). This concoction is pretty straightforward: what if you could search just the sites you wanted

Figure 11.3   LibraryThing collection page, showing covers

to, without having to wade through a lot of other stuff that shows up in your results from Google or another search engine? What if you could choose the best 15 or 37 or 1,296 sites on a given topic and have a powerful search engine look through those sites for the keywords you enter? Now you can. Here, you are mashing up the contents of these multiple sites and making them searchable through another site: a search engine. One example for doing this is the CSE service available through Google **Custom Search Engine** (www.google .com/cse). A Google CSE can include an unlimited number of URLs that are searched by the Google search engine. Another option is Blekko (http://ble kko.com), which allows you to create a "slashtag" in which you can specify a list of URLs to run a search on. Some sample CSEs and additional ways to make them may be found at Search Engine Showdown (www.searchengine showdown.com/cse).

The mashups described are all pretty straightforward; for each of them, you can go to a service and choose the data you want to mix. If you are of a more creative programming type, though, you can work more directly with the code that gives you access to the data of a given source. Many information sites offer their **APIs (application programming interfaces)** to the general public on the signing of an end-user licensing agreement. This gives the user access to needed codes from the site that make it easier to construct a mashup to exacting specifications. A selection of sites that offer APIs is available at ProgrammableWeb's API Dashboard (www.programmableweb.com/apis). For an introduction to the process of using APIs to create mashups, I suggest working with Yahoo! Pipes (http://pipes.yahoo.com/pipes), which enables you to combine data sources without knowing much programming at all or having to gain access to APIs on your own.

SKYPE

VOIP anyone? **Voice-over Internet protocol** has been around for a while—the ability to have audio communications over the Internet using your computer. The quality has improved greatly over the years, and it is now used for ordinary phone communications in a variety of communities and corporate settings. Skype (www.skype.com) is of interest as a provider of VOIP because it allows unlimited free calls between two Skype users. And this is not limited to audio communications: video calls may also be made at no charge. This may help give library staff members a way to reach niche users—for example, people who might be surprised to see Skype information on a library's "Contact Us" page. It might also lead to expanding the library's ability to serve distant users, and even to assist those users with a video exchange, without charges on either end. This certainly bears considering as we try to bring expanded services to a wider range of individuals.

PINTEREST

Pinterest (www.pinterest.com) is a popular social networking tool that focuses on collections of items displayed visually. A user can select a webpage to "pin" to a "board" in his or her account, and the user may create a variety of boards, each dedicated to a certain topic. Pinterest isolates the images on the page that was selected for pinning, and the user can select one of these images to represent the page on a board. It's a great way to gather images and be able to view them together, whether you're shopping for clothes or real estate, collecting articles about your favorite places, or comparing options for library furniture (my own fledgling effort). A selection of uses for Pinterest in libraries, with linked example sites, can be found in an article by Jeff Dunn on Edudemic at http://edudemic.com/2012/03/20-ways-libraries-are-using-pinterest-right-now.

Figure 11.4   Screenshot of Pinterest

WIKIPEDIA

Ah, Wikipedia! The bane of librarians everywhere? Not in my book, but your evaluation may vary. Wikipedia (www.wikipedia.org) is an intriguing collection of information continuously being created, modified, and updated by, well, just about anyone in the world. It takes the process of creating an encyclopedia to a whole new collaborative level. The idea is that rather than trusting an article on a topic to one or two experts, why not bring in the group mind to add currency, a broader perspective, and a greater range of details to that same information? It is, in some sense, information creation laid bare: all the discussions among contributors are saved and their edits and revisions of the original document are immortalized.

It is certainly not a perfect information source, for though high standards of objectivity and good referencing of sources is expected, there are abuses. Wikipedia does bring out excellent information on a variety of topics and certainly covers a wider array of topics than most general reference sources. Information consumers must evaluate the material they find carefully, but isn't that true for all information sources? In the end, Wikipedia brings forward a great deal of useful information, along with some questionable information, and opens new debates that can only better inform information users. An excellent infographic with statistics on Wikipedia usage, titled "Redefining Research," is available on OpenSite at http://open-site.org/wikipedia.

TWITTER

Twitter (www.twitter.com) is an interesting extension of the idea of blogging, turning the sometimes lengthy standard of blog posts into something much shorter. Often referred to as microblogging, Twitter provides an opportunity for users to sign up for a free account and then start posting brief status updates and comments—or anything else that can be said in a maximum length of 140 characters per post. Photos can also be attached to individual posts by users—a feature that Twitter added in 2010. The ability to communicate quickly and easily with others to share thoughts and image is attractive to both the poster and his or her audience. Those who follow a given user receive posts from that individual, called "tweets," on their cell phones, through IM, through e-mail updates, or via RSS. If a library could connect with an audience interested in hearing brief updates from the library, it might work quite well as an updating service. See Andy Burkhardt's article on Information Tyrannosaur at http://andyburkhardt.com/2011/04/26/how-libraries-can-leverage-twitter/ for links to descriptions of Twitter and its uses in libraries.

Twitter connects with two trends in society that appear to have great appeal: texting, which is the exchange of usually brief text messages on cell phones, and the desire to cut information exchange to the essentials in all media. If libraries can provide crucial tidbits to pass along to their interested patrons, they will find an audience.

YOUTUBE

YouTube exemplifies the Web 2.0 concept of user-driven content sharing. Many thousands of individuals use this site to share the video that they have recorded or otherwise captured. Many thousands of hours of recent news and entertainment programming, movie clips, personal productions, and even educational materials are available to be searched and commented on. Library staff members can utilize YouTube as both an information resource for their patrons and a platform to add videos marketing the library or teaching the use of databases. We live in a visual culture, and YouTube is a way to reveal what's going on out there and then participate in the process ourselves.

If we can find ways to connect with our users in and through these Web 2.0 technologies, we are embodying the premise of Library 2.0 service. Library 2.0 takes the principles and technologies of Web 2.0 and applies them to changing library service toward a more interactive, participatory, and responsive model. This idea will be explored more fully in Chapter 13 in terms of placing technologies and services on library websites.

QUESTIONS FOR REVIEW

1. Can you find an example of a mashup beyond those offered in this chapter?
2. Do you notice library patrons in your library using social networking tools? Does your library have a presence in any social networks?
3. What is your experience in using Wikipedia? Do you recommend it (or recommend against it) to library users?
4. What is VOIP?
5. What might be a benefit of using Twitter or Pinterest to connect with your library patrons?

Selected Sources for Further Information

Berube, Linda. 2011. *Do You Web 2.0? Public Libraries and Social Networking*. Oxford: Chandos.
Berube provides an introduction to Web 2.0 concepts and how they can be applied in public libraries.

Bosque, Darcy Del, Sam A. Leif, and Susie Skarl. 2012. "Libraries Atwitter: Trends in Academic Library Tweeting." *Reference Services Review* 40, no. 2: 199–213.

This article is a study of academic libraries' use of Twitter, which serves as a guide for using Twitter to inform and connect with library patrons.

Engard, Nicole C. 2009. *Library Mashups: Exploring New Ways to Deliver Library Data*. Medford, NJ: Information Today.

This book presents a collection of twenty-five essays covering various applications of mashups to library services.

Solomon, Laura. 2011. *Doing Social Media So It Matters: A Librarian's Guide*. Chicago: American Library Association.

Solomon's book is a solid introduction to social networking tools that library patrons are using and that libraries should be familiar with and use themselves.

PART III
HOW LIBRARIES PUT TECHNOLOGY TO WORK

CHAPTER 12

MEETING AND SUPPORTING PATRON TECHNOLOGY NEEDS

UNIVERSAL DESIGN AND ADAPTIVE/ ASSISTIVE TECHNOLOGY

LIBRARIES ARE ALL ABOUT PEOPLE—both the people who use its services and the people who work there. People cannot be forgotten in any discussion of technology, and the intention of this book is that the concerns and needs of patrons and staff will not be overlooked. Later chapters will address topics such as usable web design, ergonomics, identity safety, and troubleshooting patron difficulties. In this chapter, the focus turns to creating a conducive technology environment for the individuals who are using, or who we hope will begin to use, libraries. Some key areas of concern for libraries relate to patrons with disabilities and patrons who use the library as their primary access point for technology. Library staff members need to know what technology barriers patrons may face and how staff members can be open to overcoming them.

UNIVERSAL DESIGN

A very useful concept for library staff members to use when assessing their libraries is **universal design**. This concept, which began in architecture and now reaches into education and other areas, is centered on the idea of making products and services usable by people with a wide range of skills and abilities. In a library setting, this thought should cause us to ask whether our services and collections are truly available to everyone we serve. This relates not only to patrons with disabilities but also to individuals who may not be proficient English speakers or individuals who may lack knowledge in using computers or other library resources.

With respect to technology, the focus of this book, we need to examine our computers and peripherals, our websites, and the ways that we use and expect our patrons to use technologies to find, access, and utilize information. Are these uses of technology sufficiently transparent to a broad group of our patrons (or potential patrons)? How could they become more transparent? An interesting element in this comes down to language: how can we express library concepts in terms that we can expect all users to understand?

There are no quick and easy answers here, but by adopting this approach libraries can continue to improve what they offer and how it is offered. Bear in mind that transparency is not something to be achieved only through passive websites or points-of-use signage. The role that library staff members assume as teachers, trainers, and intermediaries is ever more crucial and needs to expand in a more universal direction.

THE DIGITAL DIVIDE

We live in a society ever more dependent on technology—one which requires its citizens to use that technology. Chapter 2 introduced the disturbing split we see in society of a populace that demands technology use and tools from its institutions, including libraries, and of a substantial portion of our citizenry that lacks access to technology and skills for using it. This is not to say that half the country loves technology and has it and the other half hates it and does not have it. Rather, we are a society of "haves," who *have* technology available and *have* to use it whether or not we like it, and "have-nots," who cannot use technology even if we would like to. And this is not a matter of using technology for games or hobbies; it is a matter of participation in services and access to resources from governments and the business sector.

What is the technology that forms this divide? It is computer ownership or access and particularly Internet access. A Pew Internet and American Life study shows the following results: 78 percent of American adults use the Internet, as do 95 percent of teenagers. Another 20 percent of American adults do not go online at all, and 35 percent of Internet users do not use social networking sites. The divisions grow stronger when we consider various generational, ethnic, and other groupings and their percentages of Internet access: adults over age sixty-five (41 percent); people who have not earned a high school diploma (43 percent); Hispanics, age three and older (68 percent); people who earn less than $30,000 per year (62 percent); and Americans with disabilities (54 percent) (Zickhur and Smith, 2012). Significant numbers of people from these groups are not able to participate as fully as they should be able to.

If people are getting online (as more than three-quarters of Americans do), where are they gaining access? Indications are that mobile devices are filling some gaps. The same study showed that percentages of American adults own cell phones (88 percent), laptops (57 percent), e-book readers (19 percent), and tablet computers (19 percent). A total of 63 percent of American adults access the Internet through wireless connections using one of these mobile devices. The library is filling a need in assisting users who do not have a desktop computer or who are not using a mobile device—although mobile-device users who rely on Wi-Fi connections may well be using freely available library access—or who do not have another opportunity to get online. This is certainly being done in public libraries, along with school and academic libraries. And it is certainly true that these numbers merely capture the situation in the United States, ignoring the much lower access percentages in most of the rest of the world. There are technology initiatives under way that attempt to address the global digital divide (e.g., One Laptop per Child, http://laptop.org).

What are libraries to do in response to this situation? Libraries must rise to the challenge and accommodate the needs of patrons who depend on them for technology access and assistance. This need calls for resources that libraries do not always have in abundance and for policy changes that may take time to work out to the satisfaction of patrons and staff alike. Libraries must make the case to their funding agencies that they are not just the "people's university" of old but also the "people's technology lifeline." This means more than just offering Internet access; it may mean offering word-processing for job applications or assistance in navigating the websites of government agencies. No matter their size or equipment, libraries stand as beacons and sources of hope to those who need access to technology.

ADAPTIVE AND ASSISTIVE TECHNOLOGY

It is good practice to make sure not only that technology is useful for the library's community but also that it can be used by all members of that community. This section is aimed at making sure that parts of our communities are not overlooked during this process. Members of the library community who have disabilities may require an additional level of technology to enable their use of the library. The following sections explore some of the items a library may wish to add to ensure these needs are met. Keep in mind that the sections address only the technology needed to aid patrons with disabilities; a library needs a comprehensive plan to truly serve this valuable part of its community.

Technology to Level the Field

Assistive and **adaptive technology** makes the library and its resources work for users with disabilities. The terms *assistive* and *adaptive* are applied to aids that either assist the user in accessing a library resource or adapt that resource in such a way that it becomes usable. Many of these technologies are aimed at adapting computer-based resources (e.g., screen magnification software, trackball controllers), but several technologies are available for helping with more traditional library sources (e.g., teletypewriters, recorded books). A careful assessment of the needs of those with disabilities in the community can help a library staff decide which of the following technologies are required. This assessment and the added technologies can help the library meet the requirements of the Americans with Disabilities Act (ADA). More important, it can ensure that the library is meeting its mission by providing all of its users with the information they need.

Technology for Public Computers

A standard library computer such as the one described in Chapter 4 is not immediately usable by patrons with certain disabilities, such as blindness or limited motor ability. Fortunately, many technological products are available to make computers easier to use for those with disabilities. Consider the following list a survey of products. A library may wish to focus its efforts to meet certain accessibility needs that the staff have identified in the community. On the other hand, libraries can also choose a selection of adaptive technologies to cover many bases.

Screen-magnifying software. Software that magnifies the text and images on a computer's monitor is extremely helpful to patrons with low vision. Such an application allows users to control the level of magnification of the screen to fit their specific requirements. These programs offer several options for controlling the area of the screen that is to be magnified at any one time. For example, users can magnify the entire screen at once and scroll through the entire enlarged webpage or document using the mouse. Users may also select to magnify a defined area of the screen, and they can maneuver a box-like frame around the screen to center on a specific section to magnify. Many other settings and options are available.

Screen-reading software. For those with extremely low or no vision, **screen-reading software** can extend and improve the accessibility of any material that can be displayed on a computer monitor. The software reads aloud whatever text appears on the monitor, whether it is the library catalog or another resource. Users can choose to use different voices, can adjust the speed of the reader, and can train the reader to skip certain unreadable characters or improve its pronunciation of other words. Of course, anytime a sound-producing device or software appears in a library there is a need for headphones to accompany the software.

Touchpad or trackball controllers. Marketed for patrons who are unable to use a standard mouse, both trackballs and touchpads exert less pressure on an individual's hand, wrist, and arm. For those patrons with developmental disabilities or carpal tunnel injuries these devices make computer use once again possible or more comfortable in some cases. Rotating a trackball with the palm of one's hand removes the need to grip a controller with the whole hand. Touchpads allow users to control a mouse by moving an index finger along a pad that corresponds with the layout of the monitor screen.

On-screen keyboard. For those patrons who cannot enter text using a traditional keyboard, using an on-screen keyboard may be a better option. While most library resources do not require much text entry, there is still the issue of typing out search statements for the catalog, databases, and the Internet. Even typing in URLs can be difficult or impossible for a user who cannot use the keyboard. **On-screen keyboard** software allows a keyboard to appear on the screen that a user can click on using the mouse in order to select—in other words, type— letters that will appear in a web browser or other application. This may be an excellent option for libraries who have patrons with this need. It likely would be more useful in the library environment than some of the dictation software that can be used with word-processing software.

Technologies for Other Services and Materials

The technologies just described are extremely helpful in making computers and the many electronic resources that libraries offer accessible to people with disabilities. Following are some additional technologies that can make noncomputer resources and library services easier to use.

Teletypewriter. For patrons who have difficulty hearing, a **teletypewriter (TTY)** connection can offer a means for communicating with library staff members. A TTY device is connected to a telephone at a patron's home and to a telephone at the library. Some libraries set up a separate line for this service. The device allows the patron and staff member to type messages back and forth. This can be extremely helpful for obtaining library information, asking and answering reference questions, and making other requests of library staff. Some libraries are finding that virtual reference through web-based chat or instant messaging can be an effective replacement for standard TTY devices.

Closed-captioning. DVD/video viewing station equipment should include the option of closed-captioning so that users with hearing difficulties can still make use of videos. Most televisions or television/DVD/VCR combinations include this as an option. The other half of this question is whether the video or DVD itself contains closed-captioning. This should be confirmed before an item is purchased for the collection.

Magnifiers. Book and periodical magnifiers can make traditional library materials more usable for patrons with low vision. These units have a tray on which one can place a print publication. Over the tray is a magnifier unit that displays the publication on a screen. As with the computer screen magnifier, setting adjustments are available. Another version of this technology is closed-circuit television, in which the magnifier device is hooked up to a television of any size for ease in viewing.

Audiobooks. For patrons with extremely low or no vision, recorded books in various storage formats should be made available. Wonderful work is being done by dedicated talking-book libraries throughout the world. This particular medium is an easy one to add to any library's collection. Many titles are available as audio e-books in addition to earlier audio formats (e.g., compact discs).

Kurzweil readers. The Kurzweil reader in its many varieties has had an immeasurable impact on making printed materials available to individuals with no vision. This device scans and audibly reads the information printed on a page.

Braille equipment. Braille translators and printers may also be of use to those patrons who prefer having Braille copies of printed materials. These devices require a computer set up with translating software and an accompanying printer that prints Braille characters on paper. The equipment can be quite expensive, but not many libraries need such a device.

Web and Interface Design Considerations

When approaching the design of a website or a database interface, it is almost impossible to make everyone awaiting the outcome happy. Aside from aesthetic differences, it is difficult enough to choose which features to include and how to make the site or interface easily navigable. What is important in this consideration is remembering that there are individuals using the website or databases who are not worried about the nifty images spread across the pages or the time spent considering color schemes. These are individuals with extremely low vision or no vision, who are accessing these electronic resources using screen-reader software.

An issue to consider in this situation is that there are a number of items (such as images) that are completely ignored by this reading software. Typically, people who use screen-reading software are also using a simplified, nongraphical web browser. Web designers need to take a look at how their pages display in text-based browsers such as **Lynx**. Images will not display, but in the HTML (hypertext markup language) coding used to make webpages there are **image tags**, such as captions, that will appear. Designers need to make sure important images that communicate information of some type also communicate that information through the image tags. This is but one consideration that interface designers must make. In the Selected Sources for Further Information section of this chapter, some of the listed websites can give further advice on crafting workable sites and interfaces and making sure that standards are met. Section 508 of the Rehabilitation Act (nicely explained at www.section508.gov) provides standards on web design that are now required of all U.S. federal agencies. Other community and public institutions (such as libraries) are following these site design standards as well. The World Wide Web Consortium (W3C), a web standards organization, has a page on its Web Accessibility Initiative that can help with accessibility questions (www.w3.org/WAI/).

Suggested List of Adaptive Technology for Library Computers

- Smart Cat and Easy Cat from Cirque Corporation, which are touch-pad controllers (www.cirque.com)
- ZoomText Magnifier/Reader from Ai Squared, which provides screen magnification and screen-reading capabilities (www.aisquared.com)
- OnScreen from R. J. Cooper and Associates, which is an on-screen keyboard (www.rjcooper.com)

- JAWS from Freedom Scientific, which is a screen-reading web browser (www.freedomscientific.com)

QUESTIONS FOR REVIEW

1. What is universal design?
2. Define assistive technology and adaptive technology and give an example of each.
3. Does your library include any assistive or adaptive technology?
4. Do you know of patrons who fall on either side of the digital divide? What do you think your library's role is in assisting those who need access to the Internet and other technologies?

Selected Sources for Further Information

ADA (Americans with Disabilities Act) Standards Homepage. www.access-board.gov/ada.

This U.S. Access Board website displays the U.S. government regulations for ensuring access to people with disabilities. The guidelines and diagrams found within the standards documents may be useful when setting up an adaptive computer.

CAST (Center for Applied Special Technology). www.cast.org.

CAST's website includes a variety of information on assistive technology and methods. Links are provided to webpage analysis tools that check to see how well a page conforms to W3C guidelines.

EASI (Equal Access to Software and Information). http://easi.cc.

Linking to a variety of resources on adaptive technology, this is an excellent resource for questions on making computers and computer applications available to those with disabilities.

Felix, Lisa. 2008. "Design for Everyone." *Library Journal* 133, no. 16: 38–40.

This article has a good definition of universal design and an explanation of related concepts. Felix includes an annotated bibliography on universal design and barrier-free design.

Librarians' Connections. www.disabilityresources.org/DRMlibs.html.

This DisabilityResources.org webpage provides a directory of websites on disability issues and includes a section on making library electronic resources accessible to those with disabilities.

Lubin, Jim. 2012. DisABILITY Information and Resources. Last modified September 5. www.makoa.org.

This website provides a comprehensive listing of information and products relating to a wide variety of disabilities.

Mates, Barbara T., and William R. Reed. 2011. *Assistive Technologies in the Library*. Chicago: American Library Association.

Mates and Reed cover accessibility needs in libraries and a variety of technologies and practices that can be used to meet them.

Neumann, Heidi. 2003. "What Teacher-Librarians Should Know about Universal Design." *Teacher Librarian* 31, no. 2: 17–20.

The article explains the various contexts (architecture, information access, and learning) in which school librarians should consider universal design.

Zickhur, Kathryn, and Aaron Smith. 2012. "Digital Differences." The Pew Internet and American Life Project. April 13. http://pewinternet.org/Reports/2012/Digital-differences.aspx.

This report examines differences in how demographic groups in the United States connect to the Internet as well as changing methods of Internet access.

CHAPTER 13

LIBRARY 2.0
AND THE LIBRARY

VIRTUAL REFERENCE,
BLOGS, AND USABILITY

THE WEB PRESENCE OF a library has become crucial to its success, due to the need for a gathering point for links to its electronic resources and to the centrality of the Internet as a place for people to locate information. Library websites provide the library with a space to share its services with and to tell its story to the community it serves. A lack of attention to the website is a missed opportunity for marketing, and has a negative impact on patrons looking for the information they need. In addition to the website itself, libraries must be focused on building and offering interactive services through the site. What I hope to accomplish in this chapter is to suggest some Web 2.0 tools (such as those discussed in Chapter 11) that can give a library new ways to engage, connect, and communicate with the community of users that it serves. I also think some of the questions asked in this chapter can move a library to reevaluate its internal operations and processes to gain an even stronger service orientation. One thing libraries cannot lose in our information technology–dominated age is the ability to use technology to accomplish new services.

WHAT DO LIBRARY WEBSITES OFFER?

Library websites vary as much as their libraries' buildings do. While there is no "perfect" library website model that can be copied from location to location and library to library, there are some common services and features that most sites include. Many of these options are likely to be on or linked from the homepage of the site, but some may also be grouped on subsequent pages.

Interaction with the library catalog. Users who are familiar with web-based banking, shopping, and other services have an interest in completing similar library functions online. For instance, the ability to go online and log in to one's library account to renew items or request holds is a great service to patrons. Most library system vendors make these options available to patrons through the catalog interface. Depending on your system and your library's policies, patrons at home may also be able to request materials to be held for them at your circulation desk (whether the item is located at another branch or within your collection). Links to "Renew Your Materials" or "Check Your Library Record" are common on library sites. Again, depending on the development of your library system, you may also be able to provide more of the discovery layer interface to library resources that was covered in Chapter 7.

A gateway to electronic resources. Libraries need to organize the various periodical indexes, electronic reference collections, and other databases they subscribe to so that patrons can locate them. Multiple entry points are fairly typical for resource organizing systems: (1) alphabetical lists, (2) resources organized by subject, and (3) resources organized by type (periodical indexes, encyclopedias, etc.). The key is to give users the best chance to find the resource(s) that will benefit them the most. A discovery layer search box, which was discussed in Chapter 9, is a common link on the homepage of the site because it helps users search a broader array of resources.

Accessing library databases remotely. Instructions on how to use the library's proxy server or other authentication steps are a natural fit to the library website. If users are encountering the website from outside of the library, they will need assistance in accessing licensed resources.

Library "how-to" guides or tutorials. The web provides great opportunities to place documents, screencasts, or interactive tutorials that can help users make use of the library. Both in-house and remote patrons can benefit from reading, listening to, or watching explanations of how to choose and use electronic resources, how to renew a book, etc. There are many examples of useful guides and tutorials on library sites.

Virtual reference. Though it can be conducted in a variety of ways, the intent of virtual reference is to allow remote patrons to connect with library staff members and have their questions answered. Some methods, such as e-mail, text (SMS), or instant messaging (IM), are relatively inexpensive, whereas commercial virtual reference vendor options (which often include web-based chat) may be fairly expensive. There are several choices to make, mostly revolving around how immediate or interactive the library intends this service to be (e-mail is a delayed, asynchronous technology) and when during the day the service will be offered. Regardless of the choice, virtual reference provides another way for users to connect with staff and seek their expertise. Interestingly, libraries that offer virtual reference sometimes find that in-house patrons will use virtual methods to connect with staff members who are only several feet away.

Library blogs. Blogs are mainly used to announce new resources or services at the library or to give patrons another venue to communicate with staff and provide feedback. Libraries can have a single blog with general library information or various subject-oriented blogs

Figure 13.1 Screenshot of University of Minnesota's University Libraries website

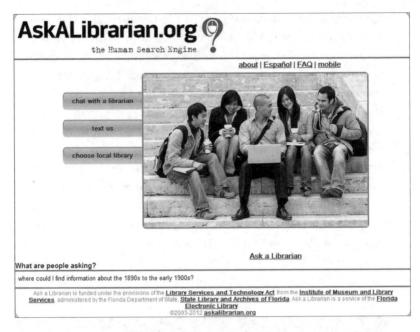

Figure 13.2   Screenshot of AskALibrarian.org reference service page

to reach different groups in their communities (e.g., for topics such as genealogy or physics). One thing that libraries are also doing is bringing postings from other blogs into their websites. These groups of postings, or **feeds**, can be gathered from the blog they are posted on using a technology called **RSS (or rich site summary)**. Libraries can in turn use RSS to make their own blog feed available for individual users to read using feed-reader software or to post on their own websites. The online diary format of blogs makes it a perfect means to keep patrons updated and to help the library distribute information in a way that does not overwhelm patron e-mail inboxes.

QUESTIONS TO ANSWER FOR WEB CONTENT PLANNING

When considering current sites and planning new ones it can be useful to ask questions to guide this process. The areas addressed in the following questions are a starting point for discussing and then creating new web content.

Who is the audience for your site? Having an idea of who you are trying to reach can help you plan the content of the site. One consideration is whether your in-house and remote users will see the same home page when they arrive at the site. In-house users will likely need quick links to certain electronic resources that you tend to use with them, while remote users may have other interests in mind (e.g., renewing checked-out materials).

How will people come to your site? Are you publicizing your site as a direct address, or is it a destination that people will come to from a page on your primary institution's site? This can influence what reference you need to make to that home institution.

What do people most want to know about your library? Based on the types of questions that people ask through other means and your best guesses, you should try to anticipate user needs and supply answers on your site.

What services can your library uniquely provide through the Internet? The services listed in this chapter, such as virtual reference, are mostly ones that can be offered only through the communication and display means of the Internet. What could your library do on the Internet that could be done in no other way? How can you benefit your community through offering these services?

What is the best way to present your information? You should consider a style, theme, or mode of organization that you will use on your main page and all other subsequent pages. Consistency will help you as you create additional pages and will help your users navigate the site.

Have you looked at your website as your audience will? A good hard look at the website from the perspective of a patron can illustrate issues and questions of terminology that a library staff member might miss. Further information about interface design and usability is provided in the next section.

Does your larger organization have any requirements about what your website should look like or any information it should contain? Many organizations have adopted **content management systems** (which allow centralized control for many design functions in a site) or set styles that are in place for every group within it. Drupal (www.drupal.org) is an open-source example of such a system that is quite popular in libraries.

Have you included mobile users? As noted in earlier chapters, the growth of mobile devices means that websites need to be useful in and compatible with various environments and screen sizes.

THE TOOLS REQUIRED FOR WEBSITE DESIGN

Just as sites differ, so too do the specific tools that website designers and maintainers use to work on them. It may also be that the library does not have a staff member who actually does the design but someone else in a larger organization is responsible for that task. I recommend that libraries either stay fully in control of their own design or at least be knowledgeable enough to pass their ideas on to a web designer. A variety of applications can be used to program HTML (hypertext markup language) and other web programming languages (e.g., JavaScript). Typically, designers will use two pieces of software: a web design application (such as Adobe Dreamweaver) and image manipulation software (such as Adobe Photoshop or Picasa).

GENERAL GUIDELINES FOR INTERFACE DESIGN

Libraries, in their sites and services, can work to improve their users' experiences through interface design. Interface design is the act of creating the way people will interact and navigate electronic resources (such as an online public access catalog [OPAC] or a website). Libraries subscribe to a large number of interfaces that we cannot alter or control (various public and staff-oriented electronic databases). It is therefore crucial that libraries take the opportunities they have to affect users' experiences with their services and resources. Website designers need to consider what they can do to make using the library even easier for their community.

Another way of speaking about good interface design is usability. Usability is the concern that users are finding what they need and able to use their sites without difficulty. This can apply as an extension of the assistive and adaptive technology of Chapter 12, but it also reaches a wider group of users. The suggestions that follow will go a long way toward improving the usability of library resources and improving interface design.

Resist the desire to tell users everything. Search screens and websites can easily overwhelm people with information if careful design and restraint are not used. Library staff love to share information with their patrons, but here care is needed. Keep the interface simple.

Seek input from users to help improve interfaces. The process of design involves lots of trial and error and can succeed only if users are asked to evaluate an interface along the way. It can sometimes be hard to get user feedback, but attempts must be made.

Look at what others have done. There is value in being creative and inventive with interface design, but seeking out existing solutions can help the process. If an interface works or appeals in some way, the principles of its design either can be applied directly to a new interface or at least can guide the new design.

A final element of interface design that bears mentioning is the need for designing websites for mobile devices. As the use of smartphones, tablets, and other devices with reduced screen size grows, there is greater potential for those individuals to connect to our websites. Library staff must be aware of what their webpages look like on these smaller screens and learn to make adjustments accordingly. The hope is for existing pages to be able to scale downward and to work well for users at any screen resolution. There is also the alternative of building an app for the library site that can be downloaded on mobile devices.

QUESTIONS FOR REVIEW

1. What are some questions to ask when designing a library website?
2. What is virtual reference and how is it conducted?
3. Which services do you think that your library's patrons are most interested in?
4. What services can libraries provide through their websites?
5. What is usability?

Selected Sources for Further Information

Chan, Christopher. 2012. "Mobile Sites Made Simple: Solutions for Smaller Academic Libraries." *College and Research Libraries News* 73, no. 5: 256–260.

Chan's article presents an overview of creating a mobile site for libraries through a vendor-provided product.

Clark, Jason A. 2012. *Building Mobile Library Applications*. Chicago: ALA TechSource.

This source does a nice job of introducing options for building mobile sites and apps for libraries and then showing the planning and development process.

Fox, Robert, and Ameet Doshi. 2011. *Library User Experience*. Washington, DC: Association of Research Libraries.

Fox and Doshi address methods for assessing web usability and offer suggestions on implementing changes to improve them; this book also takes on the larger questions of ways to improve the user experience of library services.

King, David Lee. 2012. *Face2Face: Using Facebook, Twitter, and Other Social Media Tools to Create Great Customer Connections*. Medford, NJ: CyberAge.

King outlines approaches to using Web 2.0 tools to engage library users and sustain relationships.

Kupersmith, John. 2012. "Library Terms That Users Understand." Last updated March 2. www.jkup.net/terms.html.

This article offers a wonderful set of resources collected by Kupersmith and aimed at focusing libraries' use of terminology on increasing user understanding. It offers research studies and best practices for naming and describing library resources and services.

Nielson, Jakob. "Current Issues in Web Usability." *Alertbox*. www.useit.com/alertbox.

This is a regularly posted column by a noted web design authority that offers suggestions on solving web interface design problems and gives tips on web technologies to use and avoid when designing a site.

Sauers, Michael P. 2010. *Blogging and RSS: A librarian's guide*. Medford, NJ: Information Today.

Sauers provides a guide to the process of blogging and using feeds to add content to library sites.

Varnum, Kenneth J. 2012. *Drupal in Libraries*. Chicago: ALA TechSource.

This book is an introduction to the Drupal content management system with special attention given to library website development and redesign projects.

CHAPTER 14

HOW LIBRARY
STAFF LEARN AND TEACH

SCREENCASTS, DISTANCE LEARNING,
AND LEARNING MANAGEMENT SYSTEMS

THE EDUCATIONAL ROLE of the library was immortalized in the early days of the twentieth century when the public library was pronounced the "people's university." Whether or not a given library has a formal educational program today, a key function of library staff members is to instruct groups or individuals on the use of library tools. To aid in these efforts, an examination of instructional technologies is a fitting section of this book. Technology has had a huge impact on how and where education occurs. This chapter focuses on distance learning and presentation technologies.

WHAT IS DISTANCE LEARNING AND
WHAT ROLES DOES IT HOLD FOR LIBRARIES?

Distance learning (also called online learning or e-learning in its web-based forms) can be seen as just another method for connecting learners with educational materials. While most formal education takes place in a classroom, distance learning makes it possible for individuals to participate in a learning experience even if they are geographically distant from an instructor or are unable to meet in real time with a class. The idea is that students can learn wherever they wish, whenever they wish, in an environment that requires independent work but is structured by an instructor and perhaps involves contact with other students. Several forms of distance learning (such as correspondence courses or televised and radio courses) have been practiced for many years, and all of them have involved one or more kinds of technology to facilitate exchanges and discussions between an instructor and students. Two-way communication must be available so that lessons can be sent out and feedback can be gained or questions answered.

Distance learning may occur at nearly any educational level, either in support of more traditional instruction or as the primary instructional means. Its growth as a method can create increased opportunities for libraries to experience it in one of the following three ways:

- Libraries may support distance learning by providing resources for participants. This may involve making equipment available in house or providing information sources to help students with their studies. Academic libraries may need to support classes offered by their institutions through providing access to their databases to remote students. Public libraries that offer Internet access to community users may find distance-learning students using this access to download assignments or contact instructors. They may also serve as sites for community groups to participate in videoconferencing. Whether our support is direct or on an ad hoc basis, the implications of distance learning affects many libraries of all types.
- Libraries that instruct their communities on how to use the library or its resources may well use distance-learning techniques to reach remote users or distance-learning participants. This would primarily apply to academic libraries, but other libraries may have opportunities to instruct remote users on an occasional basis.
- Library staff members may themselves participate in continuing education or professional development opportunities via distance-learning technologies, perhaps taking part in graduate and associate degree programs in library and information science. There are also a number of other courses and workshops available to staff from educational institutions or professional organizations.

Distance learning is not for everyone or for every situation. In each instance, a set of supporting resources must be available for the instruction to work. Sometimes those resources involve your library's collections so that you can help a distance-learning student find research materials for a paper or other assignment; at other times the resources might involve equipment. Distance learning has the potential to be a liberating experience for students, freeing them from the limitations of the traditional classroom and class schedule. Because there are a number of situations where it does fit the need, we are bound to see increasing numbers of opportunities becoming available.

SYNCHRONOUS AND ASYNCHRONOUS DISTANCE-LEARNING TECHNOLOGIES

Synchronous technologies are ones in which the instructor and students are involved in the learning process at the same time. Some possibilities for **real-time communication** and interaction include the following:

- An audio teleconference (like a conference call) can be used and would be relatively inexpensive. Interaction can be accomplished over the phone if needed. With some additional equipment, video can be transmitted over the phone, a process known as audiographics.
- Television can be used to send out a seminar or a class and can reach individuals in a local area cheaply and easily. Students probably own their own televisions, so little equipment investment is needed. Television grows more expensive if satellite or cable transmission is required to reach a wider audience. In these situations, it is more common to use television for brief (half-day) teleconferences that are sent to predetermined locations (e.g., schools, libraries) that can receive satellite or cable transmissions. Interaction is again possible through telephone or e-mail.
- Videoconferencing is an excellent way to simulate the live classroom with two-way video and interaction. Demonstrations of nearly any kind are possible. It is rather expensive, however, because it requires videoconferencing equipment on both ends. This is not likely to be used to communicate to a large group of individuals at separate locations. Rather, focused connections between the instructor's location and a single remote videoconferencing classroom can be used for brief workshops or full-length college classes.
- The web offers several possibilities for synchronous communications. A virtual classroom, instant messaging, or a virtual world can be used for students and an instructor to exchange information and questions. Virtual classrooms may be built within a learning management system (see the next section) or may be freestanding environments. They typically allow for multiple individuals to share images, slides, video, audio, interactive chat, and web browsing capabilities for meetings, webinars, or credit classes. An example of this is Black-

board Collaborate (www.blackboard.com/platforms/collaborate/overview.aspx). Instant messaging (IM) is another possibility for contact between an instructor and a single student. In addition to Second Life (http://secondlife.com), there are a number of online virtual worlds, environments in which several individuals can interact online in a more immersive environment. The expense of the last two of these options is typically minimal as basic access to educational virtual world space is often free and IM clients are freely downloaded. Blackboard Collaborate requires licensing of software and concurrent "seats" for participants from a vendor. Instructors and students can connect from all over the globe.

Asynchronous technologies are ones that allow delayed interaction between students and the instructor. Lessons are sent out and assignments and questions are sent back with little or no real-time interaction. Examples include the following:

- Learning through correspondence courses, which are the longest time-tested method of distance learning, involves students reading a text or separate lessons and then taking tests to prove their knowledge. There may be a little interaction with an instructor to clarify points, but typically students work when and where they wish to meet course deadlines. Much book knowledge can be communicated this way, but there is no ability to demonstrate processes or equipment in real time.
- Video-based learning involves providing to students videos or DVDs of lectures and demonstrations; the students can then watch them when it is convenient for them. It makes use of technology that students would commonly own (VCRs, DVD players, and televisions) and adds interaction by phone or e-mail. Students have the freedom to watch the instructional material multiple times to help them review the material. However, as is common to other methods of distance learning, there are few opportunities for group discussion or interaction of any kind.
- Web-based learning is somewhat similar to these other methods in that learning materials are placed on a website and students have the freedom to use them on their own schedule. Audio files, video files,

and static image files can be added to text, and participants can interact asynchronously via e-mail or web message boards.

LEARNING MANAGEMENT SYSTEMS

Any discussion of distance-learning technologies is not complete without mention of learning management systems (LMSs; also known as virtual learning environments [VLEs]), which offer elements of both synchronous and asynchronous interaction. **Learning management systems** are web-based products that provide the technological framework for wholly distance-taught or online-supplemented courses. They are often used in college and university settings as either commercial or open-source products. They offer web space to place documents and other textual course materials, as well as a central place for students to find links to other online content. In addition, learning management systems can host interactive chat sessions with multiple students and provide for the presentation of visuals as well as text. Testing and survey options are available. A major commercial vendor of these products is Blackboard (www.blackboard.com), and open-source examples include Moodle (www.moodle.org) and Sakai (www.sakaiproject.org).

As a side note, there have been some efforts in the past few years to have academic librarians interact with faculty and students in LMS classrooms. These embedded librarians take this step to be readily available to students at their point of need in working on class assignments and research. This is of particular import with students who are taking classes entirely online or who spend most of their time distant from the college or university offering the class. However, embedded librarians also work with more traditional courses that meet face-to-face but have coursework and discussions in the LMS. The librarian will typically post useful research links, web-based tutorials or screencasts, and interact synchronously or asynchronously with individual students or the whole class. Some embedded librarians stay in the course for a short time; others are present during an entire semester or term.

WHAT ARE PRESENTATION TECHNOLOGIES
AND HOW ARE THEY USED BY LIBRARIES?

Presentation technologies allow us to share information with an audience in a visual manner. Our presentations can be made more vivid and more informative by bringing in visual aids through the use of display equipment, media items, and presentation software. While there are many situations in which a verbal presentation will suffice, for many situations it would be nice to either demonstrate an activity, to show the resources that are being discussed, or to illustrate key points of the talk in a visible manner. The methods discussed in this section can accomplish these purposes.

There are three basic roles for **presentation technology** in libraries: (1) the display equipment and media items can be managed and scheduled for use within the organization that the library is a part of; (2) elements of the technology, particularly media items, may be circulated to the community at large; and (3) the use of presentation technology can be incorporated into library instructional efforts. Both patron training in library resources or services and staff training can be aided by presentation technology, as can any informational presentation.

Display Equipment

Display equipment allows a user to project text, graphics, video, or live demonstrations of electronic library resources onto a screen. While historically this equipment has included such venerable items as slide projectors and film and filmstrip projectors, today the primary means of display involves LCD (liquid crystal display) projectors. LCD equipment (often called digital projectors) can project output from computers, DVD players, television, and other items. **LCD projectors** can be mounted on the ceiling of room or mobile as part of a computer cart unit. A technology called **DLP** (**digital light processing**) is an alternative to LCD. DLP provides a much brighter image in projection but is still quite expensive for wide implementation.

Another direction for display equipment is the use of interactive whiteboards. These items connect a large-screen display with the ability to interact with presented materials by touching or "writing" on the screen. Software allows for the capture of what is drawn or written for later use (e.g., posting notes to the class). The screens resemble typical whiteboards but are connected to a computer (either a desktop or laptop) to enable the display of digital presentation materials or interactive Internet content.

Presentation Software

Presentation software—for example, PowerPoint or the web-based Prezi (www.prezi.com)—can bring together both old and new media to create a professional presentation. Each individual screen or segment of the presentation is known as a **slide**. Anything that can be produced or brought into a computer can be added to that slide: text, links to websites, video clips, sound—you name it. The programs offer templates and preset designs for new users while leaving many creative options open for advanced users. It is not difficult to produce a very entertaining and professional presentation using this software.

SCREENCASTS

Libraries might also make use of commercial software, such as Adobe Captivate, TechSmith's Camtasia, or Articulate, or free web options like Screenr (www.screenr.com), Jing (www.techsmith.com/jing.html), or Screencast-O-Matic (http://screencast-o-matic.com). With these applications, you can take presentations like those described previously and turn them into free-standing videos that can be linked from the library's website and available to patrons at any time. Articulate also lets you add sound to the presentation. Adobe Captivate and TechSmith's Camtasia and web options add the capacity to record live action work in a web browser or an office application to show users exactly how to move around in a resource. The resulting video tutorials or screencasts can prove to be powerful instructional tools. They allow users to easily review the use of a database or the process of evaluating information found on the web. A key point with screencasts is to keep them short enough (or in modular format) so that patrons can quickly get to the particular piece that they need.

QUESTIONS FOR REVIEW

1. What are the three roles that libraries can assume in distance learning?
2. What is an LCD projector?
3. Explain the difference between synchronous and asynchronous technologies, and give examples of each.
4. What presentation software do you have available in your library? Have you used Prezi?
5. Have you ever participated in distance learning? Would you recommend it to someone else based on what you have read in this chapter or your own experience?

Selected Sources for Further Information

Anglin, Gary J., ed. 2011. *Instructional Technology: Past, Present, and Future.* Santa Barbara, CA: Libraries Unlimited.
This collection of essays explores concepts within instructional technology and provides examples of teaching methods and approaches.

Burke, John, and Beth Tumbleson. 2011. "A Declaration of Embeddedness: Instructional Synergies and Sustaining Practices in LMS Embedded Librarianship." ACRL conference, March 30–April 2, Philadelphia, PA. www.ala.org/acrl/sites/ala.org.acrl/files/content/conferences/confsandpreconfs/national/2011/papers/declaration_embedded.pdf. This paper is an introduction to embedded librarianship in the LMS that provides a justification for establishing this service.

Mackey, Thomas P., and Trudi Jacobson, eds. 2011. *Teaching Information Literacy Online*. New York: Neal-Schuman. Mackey and Jacobson have edited an excellent collection of chapters on different facets of teaching information literacy skills using technology. This book covers a wide variety of current technologies that can be used for instructional purposes.

PART IV

BUILDING AND MAINTAINING THE TECHNOLOGY ENVIRONMENT IN LIBRARIES

CHAPTER 15

PROTECTING TECHNOLOGY AND TECHNOLOGY USERS

SPAM, SPYWARE, AND SECURITY STRIPS

INFORMATION TECHNOLOGY PRESENTS few physical dangers to its users, but users can be quite dangerous to technology. Unfortunately, people can steal, damage, or even unintentionally ruin the technology we (and they) depend on. While it would be an overreaction to treat each patron as a suspect and release guard dogs to roam among the stacks at night, we need to take steps to protect the technology in which we invest so much money. And to be fair, there are ways that patrons' personal information can be put in jeopardy. This chapter explores some of the areas of concern for security and some methods to consider.

Security measures are generally split between methods that attempt to secure equipment or media (e.g., cabling a desktop computer to a table) and those that attempt to secure software and electronic information resources. The first two categories in the next section, security systems/RFID and locks/secure locations, mainly deal with the former; the last two, limiting functions and electronic security, handle the latter.

SECURITY SYSTEMS/RFID

Library security systems are very common at most types of libraries and provide **physical security** for materials in the collection. While they do not protect only technology items in the library, they are an example of a technology with which library staff should be aware and familiar. Most systems are composed of a set of sensor panels (with or without gates) at all library entrances and exits. The sensors are set to detect an adhesive magnetic strip or sticker inside or on each item within the library. Items that are correctly checked out of the library at the circulation desk have either been desensitized (passed over a demagnetizing machine) or covered by a card and will not set off the alarm at the exit or gate. The systems are not without their flaws and failures, but they provide a sound level of protection for circulating and noncirculating books, media, periodicals, and other items in the library's collection.

RFID (radio frequency identification) is a related method for libraries to protect their physical collections. RFID adds something to the security strip magnetizing/demagnetizing process just mentioned. Each item in the collection has an RFID tag placed in or on it. The tag includes not only a setting which indicates whether the item may or may not leave the library but also coding which identifies the item. In a sense, it combines the actions of a bar code and a magnetic strip. But wait, there's more! The tag is easily read by RFID equipment without being seen (so no need to open a book to display the tag), and multiple tags may be read at one time. The tag consists of a computer chip with an antenna attached.

From a library perspective, RFID offers the possibility of maneuvering materials around the library with great efficiency. Patrons may take tagged items to self-checkout stations and, merely by placing a pile of items on a scanner, check them all out (the alarm system is turned off for each item to go through the security gates). When the items are returned, the tags can be recognized by sorting machinery that places books (in order) on the proper book trucks to be reshelved. Once items have been shelved in the library, shelf reading can be done with a handheld scanner, which will indicate items that are shelved incorrectly (by reading their tags, which include information on their call numbers). Inventories can be accomplished with a similar method.

The downside of RFID relates to questions about privacy and start-up costs. There are ongoing questions about the signal that the tag gives off and the content stored on the tag. While vendors and others indicate that the range of the signal is quite short (between two and twelve inches), the fear is that individuals carrying library materials could have those items become known to other people scanning for tags from a distance. There is also a fear that patron information will become stored on the tag and thus compromise patron privacy if this information is accessed (though no patron information is included in the tag). There are a number of questions yet to be fully answered about this technology, as its capabilities go beyond what libraries have typically placed on any item. The expense issue is a bit more clear-cut, as the cost of the individual tags is substantial, as is the time expense of touching every item in the collection. Despite these questions, a growing number of libraries are choosing this method of **collection control**.

A fair question to ask about security systems or RFID is whether the cost to install or replace these technologies represents a savings over the expected theft rate of materials without the equipment. A library operating with a regular replacement of stolen or missing items can do the math of these losses over the expected lifetime of the system. If, however, theft is a less regular occurrence at your library, you might be better off establishing a missing item replacement fund in the library's acquisition budget and save money in the long run.

LOCKS/SECURE LOCATIONS

For those technology items that need to be available to the public, a number of measures can be taken to secure them. Equipment such as computers, DVD players, televisions, and the like can be bolted or cabled to walls or to the furniture on which they sit. It may be a good idea to lock the case of a computer's CPU to protect internal components from theft. If a library has any items that are meant to be moved around within the building (e.g., TV/DVD player carts, computers, film or LCD projectors, CD players), these can be locked in a storage room to prevent unintended mobility. Media items that circulate need to be tagged the same as printed materials for the library's security system. Items held in staff areas probably do not require the same level of protection unless the overall security of the library building is an issue. Also, items that are easily observed from a service point may not need the same security as those hidden from view. Finally, a regular inventory of equipment or media can help ensure that items are present and correctly secured.

Another option for securing materials and equipment is restricting the public's access to them. This can take the form of having a closed collection of media items (for instance, placing all videos behind the circulation desk or another service point) or setting time limits on the use of in-house equipment (such as a half-hour time limit on public computers). It can also be applied in assigning shorter circulation periods to certain types of items that we might consider to be at risk. Care needs to be taken here so that undue restrictions do not hinder the public's use of technology. A level of restriction should be sought that safeguards equipment but gives the public ample freedom to browse collections or use equipment. Strict time limits or closed collections should be applied only in situations where prior damage or conflict would dictate their use or where they might deter attempts to elude security measures. The danger of setting too severe restrictions in the library is that while increasing them is never hard, relaxing ingrained restrictions can be difficult.

LIMITING FUNCTIONS

This method of protection involves restricting certain uses for technology rather than controlling access to it. While many types of equipment and media can have certain functions disabled by the vendor (e.g., a key lock on the paper tray drawer of a copier, videotapes that cannot be recorded over, microfilm reader/printers that will not make multiple copies of an image), the majority of solutions offered here relate to restricting computers and software. There are a number of capabilities you would rather not let the general public have on your public computers, namely deleting files, installing software, or changing the look of the operating system or software applications. Some of these limitations can be placed using restrictions available in the operating system itself. (Options differ depending on whether you are using Windows, Mac, etc.) Others will require computer security software, which can lock up both individual software titles and parts of the operating system as needed. Most security applications have both preset options for shutting down a piece of software and the ability to restrict certain functions.

The Internet has caused libraries to seek some ways to limit access to public computers. One method, mentioned in Chapter 10, is filtering software that can be used to eliminate access to a defined list of Internet sites. Software of this sort can be set up on individual computers or at the server level to control a large number of stations. An additional method of limiting Internet access is to install a filtering proxy server to stand between library computers and the outside Internet. While they can be used to restrict access to sites that some people may find offensive, often proxy servers are used to limit the access of public computers to certain electronic resources (and not full-blown Internet access). For instance, a library may decide that of their ten computers, four should be exclusively for accessing their OPAC and periodical databases while the remaining six can be used to access the OPAC, periodical databases, and the Internet. The proxy server could be set to eliminate web e-mail and chat sites as well. I tend to recommend against restrictions like this—but not in situations where computer use is high and keeping all ten machines open to Internet use means that no one can easily jump in and search the library's periodical databases.

ELECTRONIC SECURITY

Electronic security measures are also primarily aimed at computers and servers in the library. The issues libraries face with electronic security of their publicly accessible servers are similar to those faced by businesses and other organizations. Anytime you make a server available to the outside world, there is the chance that someone will try to break into it and either damage the server or use it for their own purposes. Library servers can contain all sorts of valuable data (e.g., OPAC records, library website files, personal documents), none of which library staff would like to lose and some of which they would rather no one could see (e.g., patron and staff ID numbers and contact information, subscription sources that are loaded on the library server). Libraries need to take steps to build a **firewall** between the server and the Internet so that only the information they would like people to access is available to the public and only those who are allowed to use secured areas of the server can do so. Many software options are available to accomplish this.

Wireless networks offer an extra dimension to the issue of server security. Since wireless signals will by nature travel outward from a building equipped with wireless access points, there is the potential for users outside of the library to connect to the network. While the signals can be blocked or lessened by bookshelves or other metallic objects, it is inescapable that someone with a wireless laptop could sit in your parking lot and have access. By requiring users to log in to the network and by setting up a firewall that restricts their access, their usage of the network can be controlled.

Another area of electronic security is more likely to affect public and staff computers. Computer viruses are easily distributed over the Internet and by other means and can pose even an accidental threat to libraries. Part of the reason for software that limits functions on public computers is to keep individuals from either downloading a virus from the web or bringing a virus in on a disc and running it on the computer's hard drive. Viruses are not always destructive, but they tend to be quite annoying and time-consuming. Having had to delete and reload the contents of a hard drive to rid a computer of a virus, I can tell you that there is a fine line between destruction and annoyance. Viruses can cause applications to malfunction and lock up, generating effects such as a line of text that automatically inserts itself in all of your word-processing documents. They can be written to reformat hard drives or to surreptitiously corrupt important data files.

The two greatest concerns with viruses are that (1) patrons may either accidentally or purposely place a virus on a public computer or (2) staff members may accidentally end up with a virus by downloading it or receiving it as an e-mail attachment. Viruses can be sent in e-mail as an attached file. If someone opens the file, the virus goes to work. E-mail attachment viruses are becoming more common and can easily be mistaken for a reputable file.

Antivirus software should be installed on both staff and public computers so the hard drive can be regularly scanned for viruses on **boot-up** and down-loaded files can be checked before they are run. Staff members also need to know how to react when viruses are discovered on public computers and to be aware of the dangers of viruses sent to their e-mail accounts.

Beyond viruses, the Internet is rife with opportunities for patrons to click on and download programs that hinder the speed of computers and increase the chances of identity theft. **Identity theft** is a situation where patron (or staff) information (e.g., Social Security numbers, other personal identification numbers, credit card or bank account information) are captured by a malicious party. **Spyware** can be loaded on a computer without the user realizing it, and this software can be used to track an individual's path online and record personal information, including passwords. Software such as Ad-Aware (www .lavasoft.com) or Spyware Doctor (www.pctools.com/spyware-doctor) can be used to root it out. Library staff must be sure that their antivirus software stays updated to help catch newly created spyware. They can also make use of the pop-up blocking capacity of various pieces of software. **Pop-ups** are Internet browser windows with advertisements that suddenly appear as a user loads a website. These pop-ups, annoying on their own, have been a source for spyware: if a user clicks on the ad, the spyware can start to download and install itself. Internet browsers such as Google Chrome, Microsoft Internet Explorer, Mozilla Firefox, and Opera include pop-up blocking features.

Spam is one hidden consumer of **bandwidth** that can slow the Internet access of a library if staff members are not protected from it. Spam consists of junk e-mails that are sent to multiple users and can quickly fill an individual's inbox. The bandwidth-clogging aspects of hundreds of unwanted messages funneling their way toward the library's servers are bad enough. Lost productivity from sorting through the chaff for the wheat of e-mail communication is another costly problem. If a library's Internet access comes through an outside provider, it is likely that some spam filtering is already happening. But individual users will want to check their **e-mail software** for options to deal with junk mail, including identifying certain topics or senders as automatically ignored e-mail that will be sent straight to a junk folder. Larger libraries that serve as their own Internet provider will want to consider installing spam filters on their mail servers to divert spam before it reaches staff members. There are also services that sort through an organization's e-mail before it reaches the organization's server and holds the offending mail on the filtering service's server. This lessens the impact on the bandwidth available to the library.

SAMPLE SECURED PUBLIC COMPUTER

Here is one possible set of tools you could use and steps you could take to secure public computers. Let's say you have one or more computers running Windows 8, connected to a network, and using the following applications: Google Chrome, Adobe Acrobat Reader, Apple QuickTime, and various other pieces of office software (Microsoft Office, etc.). You could use the following products and practices for security:

- Set up an admin account in Windows. The Windows operating system has the ability to set up a password-protected admin log-in to the computer that allows you to restrict nonadmin users' activities or to undo changes that users make. For instance, you can stop users from changing the background image on the Windows desktop or from altering the default printer.
- Use WINSelect software by Faronics (www.faronics.com/products/ winselect/) or a similar package. This is an example of computer security software, mentioned previously, that can be installed to limit the functions of applications on the computer. For instance, you might wish to lock out certain functions of Firefox (such as access to an e-mail client or the ability of users to set the default text size in the browser). Internet Security Barrier by Intego (www.intego.com/inter net-security-barrier) is similar software for Macintosh computers.
- Install an antivirus software package. Norton Antivirus and McAfee Antivirus are two of the most trusted names available, but there are other options. Webpages such as Antivirus Guide (www.firewallguide .com/anti-virus.htm), part of the Home PC Firewall Guide website, offer reviews and resources for protecting your computer from viruses. There are also a number of free or shareware options available.
- Set a CMOS password. The CMOS is the semiconductor or chip that runs the computer. It has a small amount of memory in it that runs on battery power. This memory holds settings for the computer that a malevolent user could access and alter during the computer's boot-up process. Setting a password for CMOS access will restrict access to basic settings on the computer that, if changed, could allow an individual to bypass other security settings.
- Place the computer in an area visible to library staff service areas and, for extra security, cable it to the furniture. The CPU case could also be locked.

SAMPLE SECURED DVD/VIDEO
COLLECTION AND VIEWING STATION

If you have a collection of DVDs and the viewing equipment, this is one picture of how security could look:

- Shelve individual DVDs behind a service desk (with the ability to search for these items in the OPAC or by browsing a print catalog of titles in a binder). Many libraries employ the same method that DVD rental stores use: display the empty cases for patrons to choose from, and then have them ask for the actual DVD at the service desk.
- Tag DVDs and their cases for the library security system.
- Cable or bolt the DVD player and accompanying television to the furniture on which they sit.
- If there is a concern about damage to the DVDs, set a short check-out period. Items could be given one- or two-hour loans so that they effectively could be viewed only in house.
- Train staff who issue media items to examine each container's contents both before checkout and after the item is returned—and in the presence of the patron, if possible. The outside of the containers or the OPAC record should list the exact contents of each box so that missing elements may be spotted immediately.

QUESTIONS FOR REVIEW

1. Name four security issues that impact public computers in a library.
2. What is spyware and how is it used?
3. What is a filtering proxy server and what does it do?
4. How are materials secured physically in your library?
5. Are there any restrictions on what users can do with computers in your library?

Selected Sources for Further Information

Earp, Paul W., and Adam Wright. 2009. *Securing Library Technology: A How-To-Do-It Manual*. New York: Neal-Schuman.

The information in this book will enable a library staff to conduct a security needs assessment and to construct a comprehensive security plan for their public technologies, networks, and servers.

Kern, M. Kathleen, and Eric Phetteplace. 2012. "Hardening the Browser." *Reference and User Services Quarterly* 51, no. 3: 210–214.

This article discusses ways to protect library patron privacy on public computers through browser settings and administrative tools.

Muir, Scott E. 2011. "Security Issues with Community Users in an Urban University Library." *Library Leadership and Management* 25, no. 3: 1–12.

Muir's article explores ways to protect equipment and systems while at the same time providing library services to a campus and community audience.

Pandian, M. Paul. 2010. *RFID for Libraries: A Practical Guide*. Oxford: Chandos.

Pandian has written an excellent book on RFID and its practical and potential benefits in the library setting. It provides helpful advice on choosing RFID systems and implementing them in your setting.

Reed, Charles. 2008. "The Right Mindset." *Library and Archival Security* 21, no. 2: 59–67.

This article suggests taking a broader perspective on physical security in libraries beyond merely protecting the materials. It is a good read for thinking about what you hope your security strategy will accomplish: what are you really protecting?

US-CERT (United States Computer Emergency Response Team). "Alerts and Tips." www.us-cert.gov/alerts-and-tips.

This webpage identifies computer viruses and other hazards that can threaten your computer and your files.

Web4Lib. https://listserv.nd.edu/cgi-bin/wa?A0=web4lib (archives).

The archives for this electronic discussion group are worth searching for more information. Many posts over the years have involved security measures of one kind or another.

CHAPTER 16

WHEN THINGS FALL APART

TROUBLESHOOTING TIPS
FOR EVERY TECHNOLOGY USER

UNFORTUNATELY, ALL OF THE technology we have discussed in the preceding chapters is prone to stop working correctly—or at all—at some point. This can be frustrating on many levels. We lose the opportunity to complete an action that is under way, as when a copier jams or our connection to a database is lost. We lose our work completely, as when word-processing software locks up and our document does not save. Our first reaction is made worse in situations where we realize we are unable to fix a problem and need to wait for **technical support**.

If you spend much time using technology, you will find that many difficulties can be solved with a few basic skills. While I am by no means downplaying the importance of technical support knowledge for an organization, I suggest that many fixes can be handled by the end user, otherwise known as "you." The goal of this chapter is equip you to troubleshoot technology. My hope is that you will learn how to solve a number of problems on your own and that you will also know when to seek the help of experts.

TROUBLESHOOTING GUIDELINES

The following is what I hope will be a useful set of suggestions for preparing to troubleshoot. Preparation is a good prescription for any activity in the library. With **troubleshooting**, one of the best ways to prepare is to be ready to do some creative thinking. That way, if your preparations and method fall through, you may still be able to reason your way through fixing a problem. Starting from that point, let's take a look at the preparations.

Gain and maintain common knowledge. Treat each problem you encounter as a learning experience and document your solution procedures carefully. There is great value in knowing you have encountered and documented a solution to a problem that recurs. It may not be possible to keep a written record of each troubleshooting situation and the solution to each problem, but it is crucial for two things to happen. First, if you are involved in troubleshooting a technology problem, make sure that you see the solution applied, even if it requires an outside expert to apply it. Second, make sure that the solution is made known to all members of the library staff. This way, you can try to build a group knowledge base and you also empower other staff members so that they can fix the situation if you are not available.

Be safe. When you first approach a piece of malfunctioning equipment, be sure that your goal is to do no harm to yourself or the equipment. Some elements of safe practices come from knowing something about the item you are working on (e.g., the paper can be removed from the middle section of the copier by lifting the green lever and turning crank number two clockwise), and others are common knowledge (e.g., do not scuff your shoes on the carpet and then touch your PC's motherboard or you might destroy or disable it with static electricity). Avoiding static electricity and always reading any warning signs on the equipment are my best advice in this area. I have burned my hand on microfilm readers/printers enough times to make me more conscious of the areas marked HOT. Another thing: you can be safe, but I cannot guarantee that you will keep your hands clean. (Any device that spews toner is bound to be messy.) Get to know your equipment, and do not be afraid of it. Read manuals and poke around. Having a fear of breaking something can really hinder your troubleshooting efforts.

Check the obvious. Some might reject this idea by asking, "How should I know what's obvious?" Here again, experience is our best guide. If you have a piece of equipment that breaks down on some regular basis, even months apart, you have a basis for obvious fixes: look for the problem that happened last time and try to apply the same solution. Likewise, if you know something about how a piece of equipment works, you can check a variety of parts that are essential to keeping it running. (Are the cables plugged in tightly? Does it seem to be getting power? Is there a paper jam? Is the projector bulb really working?) The most successful troubleshooting technique I have found is an easy one. If an electronic piece of equipment is not working, turn it off and then back on. The results are sometimes quite startling, and though you really do not learn anything about the problem from this solution, it is often extremely effective. I suggest that this technique be known by everyone in a library organization as it can be effective in so many situations. When you face a problem with a piece of technology that has never broken down before or one whose operation is a mystery to you, it is time to try the next steps.

Look for clues. Not to overstate the obvious here, but on occasion a piece of equipment or software will give off some clues as to why it had stopped working correctly. Sometimes these are very clear, as in the case of displayed error messages, and other times they can only be reached through inductive reasoning ("The paper only goes up to this point and then jams, so there must be something making it jam back in this section"). One technique I have found to be helpful is to have the patron or coworker who is having a problem with the technology explain to you how the problem began. You may be able to pick up a clue of what is really going wrong through some detail that the problem reporter provides.

Read the manual. Though they are sometimes poorly written or too brief in their explanations, the manuals that accompany technology can be helpful for finding solutions or correctly identifying a given problem. While in the heat of the moment we are probably more likely to forge ahead without reading, it can really pay to take a moment and locate any manuals or help documentation you have. We hang onto these things for some reason, right? This is the time to pull them off the shelf. Diagrams can be helpful at times, and sometimes reading about the common problems that some manuals list can be educational ("Well, it's not that part or that problem, at least. What else could it be?"). I admit I have been frustrated sometimes by the fact that the manual did not help at all, but I have vowed to never overlook this resource since I have had some successes.

Check the web. A natural supplement or replacement to any printed material we may have is turning to the web for guidance from the manufacturer or from other users. Many vendors' websites will list troubleshooting tips or frequently asked questions (**FAQs**) on solving problems. There may be help available here that never made it into the manual. The same goes for reading the archives of a vendor-sponsored web forum or a public Usenet newsgroup that includes discussions of similar problems. Someone may have already located an answer and made it available to the world at large through the Internet. Some of my favorite spots to look are the following:

- Join the electronic discussion groups listed in Chapter 3 to ask questions of library colleagues.
- Check the vendor's site to see if there are troubleshooting FAQs or user forums available. *The Librarian's Yellow Pages* (www.librari ansyellowpages.com) may be useful for tracking down a vendor's site, or you can use search engines such as Google (www.google .com).
- Google Groups (http://groups.google.com) is an excellent resource for searching archived discussions for specific technologies and problems.
- Web searches can identify user forums and support documents for specific technologies or electronic resources.

Ask for advice. There are some troubleshooting situations where we find ourselves blocked from progress. Sometimes we have truly reached a dead end and are unsure of where to turn next, and other times we wisely conclude that it is too dangerous to go further. Now is the time to seek advice from any and all quarters. The previous step can be an example of this, but now it is time to try a more active approach than browsing documents or older messages. Post a message to a newsgroup, electronic discussion group, or vendor forum. Ask colleagues near and far if they have any ideas. Exhaust any technical support options that you have. I tend to try out my free options before incurring any charges, but your need for a solution may be such that you should go to the real experts right away.

Watch the expert at work and learn. If you do get advice or direct assistance (in person or over the phone) that actually solves the problem, be sure to watch carefully and ask questions. This information can be key to building up your experience and the general troubleshooting knowledge of the library. You may learn a new technique or discover that this really is a more difficult problem to diagnose than you thought. Be a student here and pay attention so that you can be better prepared down the road.

TIPS FOR AVOIDING PROBLEMS

The following are some thoughts that have served me well over time as general tips on solving technical problems. Your particular situation may not be covered here, but one of these tips may help you in the future.

- Many problems involve paper jams or related difficulties. You should know or learn how paper feeds through all of the printing, copying, and faxing devices in your library.
- Printer memory errors are common when large documents are sent to older printers. Printers may lock up completely or they may print pages full of garbage characters and images. Know how to cancel print jobs and the correct steps to clear out your printer memory; in some machines, it can be as easy as turning the printer off and then on. If you are in a networked printing environment, find out who has the power to cancel print jobs, if it is not you, and how to clear the entire print queue (the collection of waiting print jobs) if necessary.
- Technology equipment can get pretty dusty. Dust can collect inside CPU cases and keyboards and cause them to stop working. A can of compressed air can be very helpful in these circumstances. You may wish to regularly check and clean equipment in this way. Computer mice will also pick up lint and dust and lose some sensitivity. If you have a trackball mouse, pop out the trackball every so often (look for directions on the bottom of your mouse) and shake out the foreign matter. If you have an optical mouse, make sure nothing is obscuring the LED sensor on the bottom.
- If you notice even a minor problem with a piece of equipment that is used by multiple staff members or the public, be sure to note it to other staff who might get a complaint about it. Forewarned can be forearmed in some cases, and in others it is good to pay attention to smaller issues before they grow into larger ones. There are times when library staff may not realize just how often a small problem or error arises because no one remarks on it. We cannot force patrons to make note of problems, but staff can try to do their best to get the word out to one another.
- Putting together a troubleshooting tool kit can be a useful exercise. This should at least be an actual tool kit with screwdrivers, extra screws, cleaning equipment, and other items that fit your library. It can also involve organizing your printed manuals and other help

documentation, as well as having a list or set of bookmarks of where to go for more help online. I urge you to make this collection of tools available to as many staff members as are comfortable trying trouble-shooting. The initial collection of items may serve as a point to educate your coworkers (and become educated yourself) on some good troubleshooting strategies.

QUESTIONS FOR REVIEW

1. Make a list of common errors in or failures from technologies in your library. Be sure to ask your colleagues for input.
2. What are the steps you usually follow when technology fails? Are there one or more suggested steps in this chapter that would improve this process?
3. What common technology problem in libraries is mentioned in this chapter?
4. Which troubleshooting technique is important enough for every member of a library staff to know?
5. Identify a knowledgeable technology troubleshooter in your organization and ask him or her to help you create a document on troubleshooting common problems.

CHAPTER 17

BUILDING THE TECHNOLOGY ENVIRONMENT

ERGONOMICS, INFRASTRUCTURE, AND GAMING

JUST PLUG IT IN. That's all it takes to get going with our newest technological purchase, right? Find a chair and a table, maybe, or just stick it on your desk (or maybe over there on the floor). An outlet is all it takes, right? No problem!

Well, that all depends. Each of the technologies discussed in this book has a number of characteristics: how it is used, why it might be used, and so on. What has not been covered so far are some considerations about the ability of a library building to accommodate a given technology. Some items will indeed simply plug in to a free outlet and work right away. Others will take more thought and preparation.

Beyond issues of installation, there are also some questions about using the technologies. How can the process of using technology be made as comfortable as possible? These questions have implications both for staff members and library patrons and are addressed in the next section.

PHYSICAL CONSIDERATIONS

The library building needs to be considered a technological environment. A number of characteristics about a given library affect its ability to house individual technologies. Each major characteristic is discussed in this chapter. Whether a library is starting fresh with a new building, redesigning existing space, or merely adding to that space, there are certain general criteria to examine. The most important characteristics will change depending on the technology involved.

Electricity

Does the library have the electrical capacity to handle an ever-growing amount of electronic equipment? Libraries can find themselves either adding new electronic equipment to a building that has never had it or trying to place additional equipment in a nearly overloaded arrangement. Many pieces of equipment, such as computers, can present a constant draw on electricity. A number of power-saving options are available, however, such as operating system settings in Windows or **Mac OS** that will automatically reduce processor speeds or set monitors to draw less power in periods of inactivity.

Aside from overloading a library's circuitry, equipment needs to be protected from power surges by using surge protectors. For servers or other equipment, an uninterruptible power supply (UPS) may also be needed to eliminate the effects of unexpected power losses. Using a UPS will keep equipment from experiencing the jarring effects of a sudden loss of power and will keep library systems and users from losing data. Library staff members need to consult with electricians and computer support personnel to see what capabilities are available for electrical equipment and what protective measures should be undertaken.

Heating, Ventilation, and Air-Conditioning

Can the ventilation and air-conditioning systems of the library keep the technology within from overheating? In the old days of library automation, it was easy to place the computer (or computers) in a single, air-conditioned room. Now that computers and other devices are everywhere in the library, thought needs to be given to keeping the heat down. Some equipment, such as a network server, should be treated as especially sensitive to fluctuations in temperature and kept in a separate, cool area. Still, the general characteristics of a library in terms of heat, cooling, and airflow can impact all equipment. Once again, library staff members need to consult with experts in this area to determine optimal systems and settings to keep the library comfortable for people and technology alike.

Cabling and Connections

Can the library's current network cabling support new technology devices that are purchased? Or can the library building be rewired to support a new network? These are crucial questions in this age of networked information.

Chapter 6 discussed networking options and raised the issue of adding network cabling to library buildings in which such a change would be very difficult or expensive. In these circumstances, a library may decide to use a wireless network. Just as with the electrical capabilities of the building, libraries must assess their abilities to offer access to electronic resources through computer networks. What networking capabilities are already in place and how well are they handling the needs of the library? How will the library access the Internet (e.g., via a dedicated T-1 line or by individual modems)? How many computers will have access to a resource using the Internet or a local area network (LAN)? In other words, how many computers will be drawing on a limited amount of connection speed through a dedicated line? Is it possible to connect more computers to a library's LAN (as demand for electronic resources will likely grow over time)? If an unrealistic assessment is made, the library will be unable to provide the level of access that patrons and staff will demand.

BRING-YOUR-OWN DEVICES

Given some of the mobile devices and mobile storage options that patrons have, it should not surprise library staff that they will bring these items into the library. Two key needs in this area are the following: (1) library staff need to be sure that their computers have easily accessible USB ports for flash drives, iPods, and other mobile devices, and (2) given the surge of laptops being used in libraries (thanks in part to libraries offering wireless network access), libraries need to have enough power outlets to accommodate these and other mobile devices.

Computers Equipped for Many Needs

Following up on the need for USB ports, there are other items that would make computers more helpful to patrons. Libraries should allow CD or DVD burning on their computers, much as we allow printing or copying. Also, headphones should be available for patrons to listen to audio or visual content online or to watch the library's DVDs on public computers. The profusion of content of this type, whether or not it has a research focus, means that users will be aided by this access. Many individuals listen to music or other audio materials while doing research in the library, and it is not much of an expense to add a pair of headphones to make this possible. As discussed in Chapter 13, audio content in distance learning also makes headphones helpful to distance students using library computers.

Lighting

Proper lighting is crucial for any library and can have a positive impact on the use of library technology. Glare on staff or public computers or microfilm readers/printers can be distracting. While changing the lighting system of a library may not be possible, it is a factor that should be considered when deciding where to place these types of equipment. The architecture of a given library will help dictate its lighting. Generally, lighting options should be chosen to meet the functional needs of an area of the library. Just as lights should be aligned over the aisles of the book stacks so that browsing patrons can easily see the titles and call numbers, lights over the public computer area should be placed to avoid glare on computer monitors. Where possible, staff work areas should include adjustable lighting to give staff members control over their personal workspace (i.e., adjustable lamps located at each desk or computer so that light can be increased or reduced). The resources in the Selected Sources for Further Information section of this chapter provide more ideas about lighting options.

Room and Layout

In many cases technology is engineered to be smaller with each new model of a product, but adding new technologies to a library will still impact the available space. When assigning room in a library to new devices or finding areas to shelve media, be careful not to underestimate the true size that items require. Adding technology to a library may not always call for major architectural changes to the layout of the entire library, but library staff members need to be aware there may be a need to reposition items to ensure a comfortable working environment and to let patrons easily navigate the library. Further, when technology is placed in a library, visibility is key. The new items need to be easily seen from staff service points so that they can be serviced and easily located by patrons for use. Decisions in this area, as in the others involving space, depend on the technology to be added. The technology should be placed in such a way that it does not impede traffic patterns or inhibit any functions of its own or of other devices or service points, and that it does allow for easy access and use by patrons and staff.

Furniture

The furniture requirements of new technology are another consideration, as new furniture can certainly have an impact on the room and layout issues just discussed. Here the emphasis is on user comfort, for example, providing accommodating furniture and space for users of computers or media viewing stations. In others, the question may simply be deciding where a new piece of technology should sit. While it would be nice to always be able to buy new furniture to accommodate new technology, it is more realistic for libraries to assess existing furniture first. The important step is to consider the technology's furniture need before the technology is purchased. Suggestions can then be sought from colleagues and vendors about the best way to fulfill the need.

Checklist of Physical Environment Issues

The following list of questions should be considered when adding any technology to a library, either whole new technological items or additional units of existing technology. They are not prescriptive recommendations (as all technologies will differ), but they are starting points for you to discuss with vendors and those responsible for the maintenance of your facility.

- Will the new technology have an impact on the electrical demands of the library?
- Does the new technology require any special cooling or ventilation to operate efficiently? Will its addition change the heating and cooling balance of the library in some way?
- Does the library have the necessary network or communications technology in place to accommodate a new technology, whether it is a library automation system, a streaming video database, or a new full-text periodical database? Will the current cabling system and Internet connection be able to handle this new item?
- Are any lighting adjustments needed to make the use of this new technology more comfortable for patrons or staff? Is additional lighting needed, or should current lighting be altered to avoid glare or low-light conditions?
- Will there be enough room in the library to accommodate the new technology? What may need to be moved to make it fit? Where is the most sensible place, based on its function, to put the new item?
- Will specialized furniture be needed to house the item or make it available to users? Can current furniture be adapted to the purpose or will a new purchase need to be made?

GAMING IN THE LIBRARY

A great case study for these questions and issues is the desire of many libraries to support gaming activities, devices, and collections. Gaming impacts the library in a larger way than, say, adding a new collection of graphic novels. Libraries can always figure out how to shelve new collections, and even with other media types, providing equipment may not be a huge leap (for DVDs, the footprint of a TV, a DVD player, and a set of headphones is relatively small). Though individual libraries may differ in their approaches, it is not uncommon for them to offer collections of video games for checkout as well as making space and equipment available for playing the games. This makes the technological impact on the library larger in terms of adding, supporting, and maintaining the needed game equipment and designing space for its use. Here are some questions to ask when considering making gaming a service:

- What kinds of video games do you want to add? Do you intend to add games played on computers (in which case you may be able to use your regular public computers to play them) or on console systems, such as a Nintendo Wii, Sony PlayStation 3, or Microsoft Xbox Kinect? If it's the latter, then you will need to consider where the consoles will be located and how they will be secured.
- What display options do you have in mind for using the game consoles? Even with computer-based games, you might want the opportunity for players to be able to see their efforts on a larger screen than a monitor (e.g., using an LCD projector or a flat-screen TV for a tournament). With the game consoles, you will need to add some sort of display device, especially for group play and visibility. Flat-screen televisions are an excellent addition for these uses.
- How much space will be needed for game play? Part of the space question builds from the type of display you have in mind and where you will keep the console stored (having access to electricity and wall space, for example). But a big factor in space consideration is having enough of it for actual play. Four dancers playing Just Dance 4, a popular console game, require enough floor space to move comfortably without colliding. Playing a bowling game on the Nintendo Wii requires a somewhat scaled-down approximation of the space needed to actually throw a bowling ball down a lane of your choice. It is not simply a matter of sticking a television on a table with a four-foot clearance between the table and a row of shelving. You may need

to establish a separate room for game play or rearrange open seating and computer areas to provide enough extra room. One possibility is to establish group or collaborative workspaces in the library that can accommodate small groups playing games, watching DVDs, or working together on projects.

- Will you host tournaments as part of your gaming experience? This is a very popular method of using your acquired games to promote the library and offer fun opportunities for your gaming audience. Some areas to consider include the following: (1) if patrons are asked to bring their own gaming systems, the area should have sufficient electrical outlets for the event; (2) if the tournament involves computer games, your network security should be adjusted to allow gamers to make modifications to public computer screen resolutions and to install gaming software; and (3) your tournament space must not only accommodate the people playing but also provide enough space and sight lines for nonparticipants to watch the action.

These are just a few of the possible needs to keep in mind as you consider gaming for your library. It can be a great addition to your resources and also establish "techie cred" for your library.

ERGONOMICS: THE HUMAN FACTOR

Does technology have an impact on those who use it? It certainly does. That impact can be a positive tale of efficiency and freedom. It can also be a horror story of eye strain, muscle spasms, and migraine headaches. The latter possibility is very real and as such necessitates a careful look at the ergonomics of the work and public use environment with regard to technology.

Ergonomics is all about fitting an activity to a person. This primarily relates to making people's work situations as comfortable as possible for the tasks they must perform so that they can avoid injury. These injuries can be of the repetitive strain variety (also known as musculoskeletal disorders), such as carpal tunnel syndrome or tendinitis, or can involve other conditions related to vision and headaches. While ergonomics are clearly a concern for library staff members, patrons and their use of computers cannot be forgotten. Not all patrons will spend extensive time working at a computer or reader/printer, but some will in the course of their research.

What steps can be taken to consider and positively impact the ergonomic effects of technologies in libraries?

- Ensure that the furniture in staff work areas fits the person who will be using it in terms of table height and location of the computer. For furniture used by several individuals in public and staff areas, provide adjustable chairs and keyboard heights.
- Use assistive technology where it might help. Attach antiglare screens to computer monitors to help reduce eye strain and headaches. Use **trackball controllers** in place of computer mice to reduce strain on the hand, wrist, and arm.
- Encourage individuals to take frequent breaks and to limit the time they spend on tasks that could cause repetitive stress injuries. Stretch-ing exercises can help strengthen muscles that might be affected. Remind individuals that they should stop doing anything that causes pain.

Take a look at the ergonomics resources listed in the Selected Sources for Further Information section of this chapter for specific suggestions on implementing these recommendations in libraries.

QUESTIONS FOR REVIEW

1. What questions should be asked of a new technology in terms of its impact on the physical environment?
2. Does your library offer gaming resources? Why or why not?
3. Why should libraries pay attention to ergonomics?
4. Is it possible in your library to easily see and help people who are using the technologies that you offer?

Selected Sources for Further Information

Association of College and Research Libraries. "Academic Library Building Design: Resources for Planning." http://wikis.ala.org/acrl/index.php/ Academic_Library_Building_Design:_Resources_for_Planning (wiki). This webpage hosts a collection of resources aimed at new building design and planning. While aimed at academic libraries, there are ele-ments here of use in all library settings.

Barclay, Donald A., and Eric D. Scott. 2011. *The Library Renovation, Maintenance, and Construction Handbook.* New York: Neal-Schuman. This book gives excellent guidance on issues relating to technology in library renovation and building projects, covering ergonomics as well as technical requirements.

Council on Library and Information Resources. 2005. *Library as Place: Rethinking Roles, Rethinking Space.* Publication 129. Washington, DC: Council on Library and Information Resources. www.clir.org/pubs/abstract/pub129abst.html.

This collection of essays by six authors discusses how libraries are being and will be used as physical spaces now that online information is widely available.

Gallaway, Beth. 2007. "Game On! Meeting the Needs of Gamers in Libraries." In *Information Tomorrow: Reflections on Technology and the Future of Academic and Public Libraries,* edited by Rachel Singer Gordon, 71–85. Medford, NJ: Information Today.

Gallaway offers clear justifications for the inclusion of gaming in libraries. She suggests important aspects that need to be present in a library for gaming to happen and provides guidance on how library staff should prepare.

Green Libraries. www.greenlibraries.org.

This website presents a collection of links to sample green building and design projects for libraries, as well as planning documents for environmentally aware construction.

Library Leadership and Management Association. 2011. *Building Blocks for Planning Functional Library Space.* Chicago: American Library Association.

This recent book offers diagrams of library equipment and furniture to use in designing library spaces.

Mueller, Misha. 2006. "Keep Breathing: Coping with Technology." *Library Hi-Tech News* 23, no. 5: 27–30.

The author introduces paying attention to ergonomics as a method for coping with technostress. The article suggests a variety of preventive techniques to avoid injury and stress.

Sannwald, William W. 2009. *Checklist of Library Building Design Considerations.* Chicago: American Library Association.

Sannwald offers several focused chapters on elements of design and building considerations in libraries.

Utah State Library. 2012. "Planning and Building Public Libraries." http://library.utah.gov/programs/development/toolkit/index.html.

This webpage offers a collection of links to vendors and projects relating to the construction and equipping of libraries.

PART V

WHERE LIBRARY TECHNOLOGY IS GOING AND HOW TO GET THERE

CHAPTER 18

WRITING A
TECHNOLOGY PLAN

HOW CAN YOU OFFER enhanced services in your library? How can you prepare to afford forthcoming technologies? How can you be sure you will have staff members with the skills needed to implement them? Without at least some advanced planning, you simply cannot. Planning is sometimes looked at as a waste of time, or a chance to dream a bit, put some ideas on paper, and then file them away. A **technology plan** is not a static document. It is an attempt by a library to take inventory of its current technology, survey the needs of its users and its staff, and make a plan to acquire technologies to meet these needs.

Your technology plan needs to be a flexible document. It can be a very specific, short-term list of equipment that needs to be purchased to meet current service needs. It can be an inventory of current equipment that serves to create a long-term replacement schedule. It can be a mixture of current and future needs, including both easily attainable and wish-list goals to acquire new technology. Again, the plan is not set in stone; it is more of an ongoing process to assess and meet needs. Brainstorming is required.

There are many fine technology plans and planning processes to use as models when creating your plan, but do not feel so tied to one that you ignore the specific needs or characteristics of your organization. No two technology plans are alike, nor should they be. On occasion, you may find that a particular funding agency will require a certain type of technology plan, and in those cases you will have to try to accommodate the agency's needs to qualify for funding.

TECHNOLOGY PLANNING STEPS

How does a technology plan come together? The following list of seven steps provides an overview of the process and the key tasks to complete. There are a number of books and websites that offer more detailed processes, and these are listed in the resources section.

Step 1: Inventory Your Current Technology

Start by determining what technology you already have. It may be a count of equipment, or media types, or both. This process serves a number of purposes. First, you get an idea of how up to date and functional your current technology is. You may realize from your inventory that you have a number of items that should be upgraded or replaced in the near future. Second, you may discover technologies that you did not realize you had (software, older media types, peripherals, etc.). Realizing that these items exist may lead you to new uses for them. Third, you can refer to the inventory to check for gaps in your technology holdings that you had not recognized before. You may generally know what you have and what items are needed in your library. However, in instances when you decide to add new technology, without a full inventory in place you may overlook the cost-saving fact that you already own a part of the items you need. Replacement, reallocation, and recognition of gaps are all crucial benefits of an inventory.

Step 2: Conduct a Needs Assessment

Next, think about what needs you have that technology could meet. There are times when simply adding more of existing items (DVDs, computer **workstations**, etc.) will do the trick, and other situations where entirely new approaches to technology must be taken. Encourage staff members to attend technology exhibitions, new product expositions, and conference seminars on cutting-edge technologies. Then take a hard look at your current situation. Be sure to ask your patrons. Those who are using your library can give you some insight about what items you may still need to add or alter.

I mentioned the need to brainstorm earlier in this chapter. This is where brainstorming should happen in earnest. Consider needs you may not have thought of before. As you assess your needs, keep an open mind. There will be a later stage where you will need to prioritize your needs and provide justifications for them. Your assessment at this stage can be based on both hard facts and on perceptions.

Step 3: Investigate Your Options and Opportunities

Once you have some new technology uses or whole new services in mind, you can turn to technology information sources to research your options. Chapter 3 outlines a number of resources to use when searching for advice, comparing similar products, or investigating a given technology. This process should be focused on the ideas you formed in the previous step but should still be one where new ideas and concepts are allowed into the mix. You may encounter a completely new solution to a need only after you start investigating the available options. Likewise, you may determine that you want to follow another library's example and implement a new service you had not considered.

Step 4: Set Priorities and Make Justifications

Now comes the time to hash out the importance of each change or addition you have suggested. Take the options you were in favor of during the previous step and make the best case you can for each idea. Be sure to also note the negative points of each change. Then decide which ones have the most merit in terms of the immediacy of the needs they will fill and the ability you have to bring them into being, both fiscally and operationally. This is also the point at which you can clearly articulate the benefits of the changes you are planning. Justifying the changes will help you decide priorities. With a clear list of changes organized by priority, you now have a sense of the timeline in which you can implement the technologies.

Step 5: Create a Budget

With so many technology changes, in most instances the deciding factor for when or whether something happens is money. Having organized your list of options by priority of need, now is the time to price them out. Consider all of the equipment or media costs involved, as well as the needed staff time to install the technology, train and be trained on it, and handle any other incidental costs. You can also think about what funding you can expect in the near future and whether there are additional funding sources to pursue. You may be in a situation where the only way to afford your high-priority items is to seek grant funding. On the other hand, you may not have additional options, in which case you can use the budget process to help finalize your timeline.

It is crucial to allow some room in the budget for innovation—or, more honestly, for trial and failure. If at all possible, having some funding for projects or technology implementations that carry some risk should be built in. This gives you some freedom to experiment or to take on a newly developing technology and see what you and your patrons can do with it. You do not want to be so structured that you miss out on the opportunity to bring something into being of great value and use to your library community.

Step 6: Develop a Timeline

Once you have worked out the details you should be ready to move ahead with your plan as funding and other resources allow. At this point you should establish a timeline for the projects you would like to undertake. This can be rather straightforward if your technology planning process involves a single project or a few short-term projects. It can be more difficult to juggle a large number of projects over, say, a ten-year period. Bring together your best guesses and estimates of when you can afford your changes and realistically implement them. Create a document that is specific enough to get started on immediate goals and projects (or ones that require a long lead time) and gives some guidance regarding all of your prioritized items. Keep in mind that you are writing a plan that can be altered as circumstances require and solidified as target dates near.

Step 7: Plan to Evaluate

One step that is needed before you actually purchase new technologies is making a plan to evaluate them. I discussed evaluating technology for purchase, but next you must evaluate how successful the technology is once it is implemented. Is it accomplishing the goal you have set for it? Are your users actually using the technology? The idea here is to come up with some way of assessing the technology that will guide you in making adjustments to your current situation and in making future plans.

QUESTIONS FOR REVIEW

1. Does your library already have a technology plan?
2. How well is your current technology meeting patrons' needs?
3. What would you like to see added to your library over the near future?
4. Follow the steps suggested in this chapter to inventory your current technology, conduct a needs assessment, and so forth.

Selected Sources for Further Information

Cohn, John M., and Ann L. Kelsey. 2010. *The Complete Library Technology Planner: A Guidebook with Sample Technology Plans and RFPs on CD-ROM.* New York: Neal-Schuman.

> This book provides information on creating technology plans for every type of library, and the accompanying CD-ROM includes a variety of sample plans and RFPs.

Matthews, Joseph R. 2004. *Technology Planning: Preparing and Updating a Library Technology Plan.* Westport, CT: Libraries Unlimited.

Matthews presents organized processes for creating technology plans. This book offers good use of illustrations and good organization in a slim volume.

Mayo, Diane. 2005. *Technology for Results: Developing Service-Based Plans.* Chicago: American Library Association.

This book presents a series of customizable worksheets intended to guide the reader toward developing a technology plan.

TechSoup for Libraries. 2009. *Joy of Computing: Planning for Success.* www .techsoupforlibraries.org/cookbooks/planning-for-success.

This "cookbook" compiles suggestions on public library technology planning and implementation from more than 100 librarians—and it's free as a PDF download from this webpage.

WebJunction. "TechAtlas." www.webjunction.org/explore-topics/techatlas .html.

This webpage has links to documents on various aspects of the planning process and also links to the TechAtlas planning tool. TechAtlas provides technology inventories and staff surveys and assessments along with a budget worksheet.

CHAPTER 19

OUR TECHNOLOGICAL FUTURE

RANGANATHAN MEETS GOOGLEZON

THE FUTURE OF LIBRARIES, much like their history, is impossible to consider without talking about technology. Chapter 2 clearly shows that the history of libraries is a story of technology. When we think about the future of libraries, we need to approach the question much as we might approach the future of information technology. What technological developments in the world at large may impact libraries? What are libraries doing on their own that may affect their services and improve how they do business? Here are a few issues, trends, and predictions to provide a sense of what the future may hold.

NEW CHALLENGES

Some have suggested that as the Internet rises as an information source and communications mechanism, it may eventually replace libraries. It can easily be argued that the Internet lacks many of the information sources found in libraries and has no one to provide the services of libraries. However, as information on the Internet continues to grow in volume and quality and reaches a wider audience, how much longer will those objections be accurate? Four movements in our current society have started us down a road where it is less clear what libraries do that is distinct: (1) bona fide fee-based information resources appear on the Internet as free services—*The Christian Science Monitor* (www.csmonitor.com) and the *Information Please Almanac* (www.infoplease.com) are but two examples; (2) online reference question answering services are maintaining services, both nonlibrary services such as Yahoo! Answers or AllExperts.com and free Ask-a-Librarian services such as the one available through the Library of Congress and just about every public and academic library around, not to mention the prevalence of people using search engines to find answers; (3) web organizations or groups of individuals could even take on the library's role of organizing information, and some would argue this is already happening with search tools, Wikipedia, and elsewhere; and (4) Google and Amazon are providing the ability to search and use free collections of full-text books that are either free of copyright restrictions or that have been licensed to the companies—and all in addition to e-books that these vendors conveniently sell on the same sites.

One interesting look into the future that suggests where search engines and other online sources may take us involves two of the web services covered in Chapter 10: Google and Amazon. Released in 2004, a mock newscast set in the future (which can be viewed at www.robinsloan.com/epic/) shows the events leading up to the formation of "Googlezon," a corporate conglomeration of information services that takes over the world in 2014 with a personalized news and information service called EPIC (Evolving Personalized Information Construct). All information content is produced by individuals, not the press or media corporations, and then rewritten to fit the interests and specifications of each individual in the world. As the media disappears, and information becomes so subjective and individualized, will there be a place for libraries to even archive some subsection of the information?

In a lot of ways this prediction missed out on some elemental changes in the past decade: the advent of Facebook, mobile devices, etc. We could argue that Facebook is EPIC in part (an individualized space, with ads and news stories tailored to each user's profile). Many of the predictions have happened, and others still await us. I am not saying that the web will replace libraries or that it is already starting to, but I do find it difficult to ignore these trends—and some potential futures that they point toward. We may well see libraries change to virtual, rather than physical, locations much more quickly than I would have imagined.

PREDICTING THE FUTURE

Predictions are a lot of fun. We start with something we know well and then try to take logical steps to leap ahead into the future. What we end up with is at once magical and unrealistic and wonderful and perhaps horrible. As examples of this process, I offer two interesting predictions involving technology and libraries that were made more than a century apart. One has already been proven (or at least tested), while the other has either already happened (or not) or has not quite two decades to go before we can fully evaluate it.

The estimable Charles Ammi Cutter, library innovator, made a speech at the 1883 American Library Association Conference in Buffalo, New York (Cutter, 1883). The entire address recounted his imagined visit to the Buffalo Public Library 100 years in the future, in 1983. In it, Cutter predicted devices similar to fax machines, a huge library collection, thermostats to control heat and ventilation, and a method for sharing print catalog information among worldwide libraries, all of which existed in 1983. Not so successfully, he imagined a library that employed a huge staff (including uniformed pages), had drastically cut the circulation of fiction titles (an evil of the day), and offered public readings of books via a "reading machine."

A modern prophet, Ray Kurzweil (1999), inventor of the Kurzweil reader and many other bits of technology, offered the following predictions in one of his books. By 2009, Kurzweil expects that wearable computers will be common and inexpensive, and that most text will be created by voice-recognition software. In another ten years, in 2019, he states that paper books and documents will rarely be used; by 2029, visual and aural implants will allow humans to connect directly to a worldwide computer network that would put the web to shame. Sound crazy?

Here we see two different predictions at either end of their life spans. Cutter's vision of a future library shows that it is possible to predict general developments and even be dead-on about some things that would have seemed outrageous at the time. However, some visions that he had were clearly more fitting of his time, showing us that it is difficult to entirely leave behind our present-day understandings. The predictions we make can be trapped by our understandings of technology or processes and can keep us from making the right jumps to completely imagine new technology. Cutter wrote his speech after the invention of the telephone, and he was able to predict that telephone lines could carry data as well as voices. However, he had no context for imagining computers. Likewise, it is difficult for us to imagine new processes that might be invented and implemented in the future, so it is therefore difficult for us to even come close to predicting the changes that will take place.

Kurzweil's view of the near future needs to be treated with the same caution. His leaps are similar to those of Cutter in that they follow known technologies. Wireless computers and cell phones are here now and growing more widespread; wearable computers are readily at hand in the form of tablets and smartphones; we can use voice-recognition software; there are already documents produced in only electronic formats; there is a worldwide computer network. Kurzweil is taking the known and making it more universal and also letting some technology jump ahead much in the same way technology as a whole jumped ahead during the twentieth century. Cutter's vision is familiar today, but we will have to wait and see if Kurzweil's will become so. As someone who plans to be gainfully employed in libraries beyond 2029, I am interested to see how close he comes.

TRENDS AND TECHNOLOGIES TO WATCH

Looking toward the future allows us to see what is happening right now and project what the future may hold. The following list of trends and issues involving technologies is not complete, but it is designed to be suggestive of what is happening now in libraries and where libraries are going. Some of the items on the list have been influenced by the Library and Information Technology Association's (2012) list of technology trends, which is available from their website.

- Libraries' move to add electronic sources has caused a tremendous reliance on them. The ability of libraries to continue to afford electronic sources could seriously decrease their purchases of print, microformat, and physical media resources, absent significant budget increases.
- The influx of many more electronic sources has made well-designed, aesthetically pleasing library websites crucial for accessing them. If we cannot get our users to the resources we offer, we are wasting our money and their time.
- Patrons still desire interaction with the human face of the library: its staff. Library staff members need to continue to find ways to aid individuals in house and remotely that maintain the high level of service our patrons expect and provide relationship-building moments.
- E-books and digital reference resources are ever-more available. It will be interesting to see what impact this has on print publishing as a whole and whether libraries will continue purchasing these resources. The continuing growth of mobile devices and e-readers, and the ability to download e-books and audio e-books to them, means that libraries will need to pay attention to developments among these devices. Doing so will ensure that we can provide materials in the formats that these devices can handle.
- Blogs and Twitter continue to have an impact in the creation of news and opinion sources by individual "citizen journalists." Will this phenomenon grow into the creation of source materials that libraries will feel called on to locate for patrons and perhaps archive? How can

libraries improve the organization and searching of blog posts and tweets, as the Library of Congress has taken on for Twitter's archives? There are great opportunities here.

- Folksonomies will continue to develop in various forms online. Libraries will need to decide if user-supplied descriptive terms can be added to our controlled vocabulary systems (OPACs, periodical databases, etc.) and study whether such additions aid patrons in finding information. OCLC has taken steps in this direction with WorldCat .org, in that registered users may tag individual catalog records.

- Full-text periodical databases and electronic reference sources are growing in number and scope. These trends have driven print periodicals and reference sources out of many libraries. How will the rise of e-books impact the collection development decisions at libraries? Will **patron-driven acquisitions** lead to collections that better fit the needs of our patrons or end in the loss of unknown but needed sources?

- Computer hardware appears to be getting relatively cheaper while some software is getting more expensive. This trend, if it holds, could allow more individuals to purchase computers or mobile devices and gain access to the Internet (for which software and accounts are relatively inexpensive). Meanwhile, libraries may find the services of their automation system and database vendors growing more expensive. Will this lead more libraries to open-source solutions?

- Increasing bandwidth is allowing more data to be moved along the Internet and into individuals' homes. Related to this are the growing availability of wireless networks and the ever-expanding capabilities of cell phones and other mobile devices. These changes will encourage even more individuals to access information from beyond the library, making remote patron authentication and the provision of digital reference services an even greater priority for libraries.

- Libraries are forming and joining consortiums and co-ops. This leads to increased access to informational resources for library patrons at a lower cost to their libraries. It can also lead to decreasingly unique collections of electronic resources as libraries can offer only what is decided by the consortium.

- Libraries and library staff need to stress their abilities to help patrons evaluate the information they find on the Internet and elsewhere. Patrons often have too many choices of information sources and need help comparing them.

- Full-text sources of all kinds are affected both by copyright issues and the unwillingness of some publishers to make their sources available at reasonable prices (or at all). Solving the copyright questions that these sources raise could mean that e-books and other electronic resources would become more widely available—as long as the issue of digital rights management for digital audio is solved alongside copyright concerns. Also, the current fluid nature of full-text periodical and reference sources could be controlled. Libraries would not have to fear titles being pulled from a database by publishers.
- As costs decrease, libraries are likely to install RFID in greater numbers and make use of its related services (automated sorting, inventory control, self-checkout). Staff may benefit from fewer repetitive motion injuries (due to decreased handling of materials during checkout). The jury remains out on whether patrons will use self-checkout in large numbers or will demand attention from staff members. Expect privacy concerns to be discussed more widely (and eventually fully addressed) as the technology gains wider use.
- As the library become less a storehouse for books and less the only physical space in which to search information tools, new purposes will be sought for the library's space. Many imagine the library continuing as a community hub—a place for individuals to gather and discuss, study, and exchange information. Others see the library developing into a space for people to create things. The library as **hackerspace** or **makerspace**, where technology tools are available for interested community members to create audio, video, or physical items, is a concept being brought to reality in a number of places. Will it remain a viable use of libraries?
- While library staff members are used to assuming technology management, installation, and troubleshooting tasks in addition to their regular duties, the need for dedicated technology staff members will grow. This is perhaps more of a wish than a trend, but the dependence of libraries on information technology is going to make the lack of such personnel more difficult to justify. Even in smaller settings, a technology-predominant position will become common. In larger libraries, existing technology units will grow in staff members as well as importance. These units are crucial not only for the skills they house and the tasks they undertake but also as a crucible for new technology investigation.

THE COMPLEX LIBRARY

Today and for the near future we will likely have what might be called a complex library: an amalgamation of various types of media and information sources, and also a combination of traditional services with new opportunities to help people collaborate in our space. Traditional print sources and electronic sources will continue to be added to libraries. The need to integrate the use of these sources will also continue. As long as libraries can offer value-added services unlike those of other organizations or individuals, there will always be a place for our work. Libraries need to stay rooted in their essential functions and societal expectations (providing access to information) while reaching toward amazing changes (such as truly virtual libraries that provide a wealth of resources over the Internet). The potential advancements and adaptations are rather exciting. With this combination of tradition and ongoing experimentation and development we fulfill the intent of S. R. Ranganathan's Five Laws of Library Science (1963):

1. Books are for use.
2. Every reader his book.
3. Every book its reader.
4. Save the time of the reader.
5. A library is a growing organism.

QUESTIONS FOR REVIEW

1. What changes do you see in the immediate future for libraries? How about further down the road?
2. Watch the EPIC 2014 video. What strikes you as possible or already present within this forecast of the future, and what seems improbable? What do you think is coming in the years ahead?
3. Look at the list of trends and note if any of these are already impacting your library or libraries around you.
4. Build the future. I wish you the best!

Selected Sources for Further Information

Cleyle, Susan E., and Louise M. McGillis, eds. 2005. *Last One Out Turn Off the Lights: Is This the Future of American and Canadian Libraries?* Lanham, MD: Scarecrow Press.

This collection of essays examines various elements of the future of libraries: the web, the library as place, pushing to the desktop, certification, and the future of associations.

Cloonan, Michele V., and John G. Dove. 2005. "Ranganathan Online." *Library Journal* 130, no. 6: 58–60.

This article examines Ranganathan's laws and applies them to the digital library environment.

Cutter, Charles Ammi. 1883. "The Buffalo Public Library in 1983." *Library Journal* 8 (September/October): 211–217.

This forward-looking article describes the author's imagined tour of a future library.

Kurzweil, Ray. 1999. *The Age of Spiritual Machines: When Computers Exceed Human Intelligence.* New York: Viking.

This book provides a vision of expanding artificial intelligence and the eventual combination of human and machine intelligences.

"LITA [Library and Information Technology Association] Top Technology Trends." 2012. *LITA Blog* (blog). http://litablog.org/category/top -technology-trends/.

A biannual positing of the most important trends and developments in technology that are impacting libraries.

Ranganathan, Shiyali Ramamrita. 1963. *The Five Laws of Library Science.* Bombay: Asia Publishing House.

This book includes Ranganathan's now-classic statement of his philosophy of library science. For an interesting update of his rules, see Cloonan and Dove (2005).

Sapp, Greg. 2002. *A Brief History of the Future of Libraries: An Annotated Bibliography.* Lanham, MD: Scarecrow Press.

Sapp presents a catalog of library-related futuristic predictions made between 1978 and 1999.

Torrone, Phillip. 2011. "Is It Time to Rebuild and Retool Public Libraries and Make 'TechShops'?" *Make: Technology on Your Time* (blog), March 10. http://blog.makezine.com/2011/03/10/is-it-time-to-rebuild-retool -public-libraries-and-make-techshops.

This article discusses the concept of a hackerspace and how public libraries could become spaces (or at least include spaces) for people to create things.

GLOSSARY

abstract: A brief summary of a periodical article; often found in electronic periodical databases along with article citations and sometimes the full text of an article.

adaptive technology: Technology used to adapt other technological equipment for use by people with disabilities; somewhat synonymous with the term ASSISTIVE TECHNOLOGY.

ADSL: *See* ASYMMETRIC DIGITAL SUBSCRIBER LINE.

API (application programming interface): The rules and code needed to create mashups by hand.

application: A general term for a piece of software or a program that can be used on a computer (e.g., word-processing applications or Internet applications).

assistive technology: Any technology that can be used to help people with disabilities find and use the information they need; somewhat synonymous with the term ADAPTIVE TECHNOLOGY.

asymmetric digital subscriber line (ADSL): A method for connecting to the Internet over standard telephone lines that allows for transmission speeds between 1.5 and 9 megabits per second (Mbps).

asynchronous: Refers to technologies used for communication or instruction that do not work in real time (e.g., e-mail or correspondence courses); users of these items send out a message and then must wait for a response.

audiocassette: An audiovisual or media format for recording sound for playback; consists of magnetic tape that advances between two reels in a plastic case.

audiovisual items (or audiovisuals): Items in a library collection that utilize sound or visual images or both (e.g., compact discs, videocassettes, audiocassettes).

authentication: The process of ensuring that an individual has the right to use a database or other electronic resource.

bandwidth: A term referring to the capacity of a data transmission mechanism, such as a telephone line or a coaxial cable, to transmit data; the less bandwidth a mechanism has, the slower it will transmit data.

bibliographic utility: A company that makes a database of cataloging records in MARC format available to libraries at a subscription fee (e.g., OCLC).

bit (b): The simplest level of computer information; a bit can have the value of 0 or 1.

bits per second (bps): Common measurement of data transmission through modems or computer networks.

blog (or web log): An online diary or journal in which an individual or a group can post entries about topics of interest; the postings are typically arranged in reverse chronological order.

boot-up: The starting process of a computer in which the computer determines whether its components are in working order and starts its operating system running.

broadband Internet access: Using DSL or a cable modem to access the Internet; much faster than using dial-up Internet access using a standard modem.

browser software: An Internet application that allows users to view websites (e.g., Google Chrome, Microsoft Internet Explorer, Mozilla Firefox, and Opera).

bulletin board: A method for communicating online in which messages are posted on a webpage to be read and replied to by others.

byte (B): Eight bits, which is enough memory to represent a single alphanumeric character.

cable modem: A device that uses the coaxial cable laid for cable television to provide users with Internet access speeds up to 2 megabits per second (Mbps).

card: A device that can be plugged into the central processing unit of a computer to accomplish a particular function (e.g., a sound card allows sounds to be played on the computer and heard through speakers); other examples include video cards and modems.

card catalog: A paper-based method for organizing the materials owned by a library, invented in 1791 in France, in which individual cards are filed for each item, and the cards are typically arranged by author, title, and subject; also known as print catalogs, these are now being replaced by online catalogs.

CD: *See* COMPACT DISC.

CD-ROM: *See* COMPACT DISC READ-ONLY MEMORY.

CD-ROM drive: A device used to read the information or run an application stored on a CD-ROM disc.

CD-RW drive: Device that allows a user to place computer files on a blank CD-R or CD-RW disc.

central processing unit (CPU): The part of a computer that contains the main working components of the system, including the RAM, the motherboard, and the computer's processor.

chat: A method for online communication in which individuals type messages back and forth to one another in a text-based, real-time exchange.

classification system: A method for organizing a library collection so that it can be browsed by subject; examples include the Dewey Decimal Classification System and the Library of Congress Classification System.

client/server: A computing concept in which a user's computer (the client) can make use of an application or resource based on another computer (the server); this concept underlies the workings of the Internet.

cloud computing: Relying on software and file services that we access through a web browser rather than as an application installed on a local network or on a hard drive; files and the means for creating and editing them all sit on the web somewhere and can be accessed by end users with a variety of devices.

coaxial cable: A type of cable used to connect workstations and other devices in computer networks; particularly good for transmitting large amounts of audio and video (as in cable television networks, which use coaxial cable).

collection control: The maintenance, organization, and growth of library collections using technological devices (in the context of this book).

collection development profile: A picture of the collection development needs of a given library (or part of a library) that can be configured in an electronic acquisitions system to shape the selection of materials through that system.

compact disc (CD): A disc that is 5.5 inches in diameter and is used to hold up to 74 minutes of audio recordings.

compact disc read-only memory (CD-ROM): A disc that is 5.5 inches in diameter and can be laser-pitted to hold up to 600 MB of electronic information.

consortium: A number of libraries that agree to work together to seek group pricing for electronic resources and may also participate in sharing their resources among other members of the group; just one term for this sort of cooperative arrangement among libraries.

content management systems: Software that is used to manage large websites by providing a consistent interface to pages and assisting in the organization and searching of documents.

copy cataloging: The process of creating a catalog record for a new item in the collection by taking an already-produced MARC record for the item and modifying it as needed for local use; this differs from original cataloging, which involves creating a new record from scratch.

CPU: *See* CENTRAL PROCESSING UNIT (CPU).

custom search engine: A search engine populated with source material and websites of the creator's choosing; a refinement of a general purpose search engine.

data: A descriptive term for information held in electronic format; data may be a text document, an image file, a file written in a computer programming language, or an audio file, among other possibilities.

database: A method for electronically organizing information in a way that it can be easily searched and retrieved; databases consist of a collection of records, which are made up of a number of fields, each of which contains a piece of information.

database software: An application that allows you to create your own databases for a variety of purposes (e.g., Microsoft Access).

demand-driven acquisitions (DDAs): *See* PATRON-DRIVEN ACQUISITIONS (PDAs).

desktop: The interface for the Windows operating system, where one can interact with applications using the mouse and keyboard; also a term for a standard personal computer (CPU and monitor) that are typified by fitting on a desktop.

dial-up connection: The method used to connect to an online catalog or the Internet using a modem to dial a phone number and connect to a modem at a library or an Internet service provider.

digital light processing (DLP): A technology for producing digital projectors that results in much brighter images than is possible using LCD projection.

digital rights management (DRM): Technological means used by content providers to protect their material from copying or alternative use beyond what they specify in license agreements.

discovery layer: An interface to library resources that allows for combined searching and display of library catalog searches alongside periodical database results and those from other electronic resources.

distance learning: A method of teaching and learning that makes it possible for individuals to participate in a learning experience even if they are geographically distant from an instructor or are unable to meet in real time with a class.

domain name: The alphabetic name given to an Internet site in place of its numerical Internet protocol address (e.g., www.yahoo.com rather than 129.137.146.1).

DSL: *See* ASYMMETRIC DIGITAL SUBSCRIBER LINE.

dumb terminal: *See* TERMINAL.

DVD: A disc that is 5.5 inches in diameter and that can be used in hold audio recordings (up to 50 hours per disc) and video (DVD video can hold between two and eight hours of high quality video); DVDs have much larger capacities than CDs or CD-ROMs and run much faster.

DVD-ROM: A disc that is 5.5 inches in diameter that can be laser pitted to hold between 4.7 and 17 gigabytes (GB) of computer data.

DVD-ROM drive: A device which, when installed in a computer workstation, can play either DVD-ROMs or CD-ROMs.

DVD-RW drive: A device which, when installed in a computer workstation, can be used to record data onto a DVD for later use.

e-book (electronic book): An electronic version of a book that may be read via the web on a computer workstation or using a mobile device (e.g., an e-reader, an iPad, or a smartphone); there are also audio e-books that can be listened to on a computer workstation or using a mobile device.

electronic discussion list: An e-mail-based method for holding discussions with many other individuals on a topic of interest; each message in the discussion is sent out as an e-mail message to each person who subscribes to the group.

electronic reference source: A source of information in electronic format (e.g., web-based periodical databases) that can be used to meet users' reference information needs.

electronic resource: Any information source that is found in digital format; this can include electronic reference sources, Internet sites, e-books, and e-journals, among others.

electronic resource management system: A module for a library system that assists the library in keeping track of its electronic subscriptions to periodicals and other online resources.

electronic security: Using software-based means for securing library workstations and servers to protect against viruses, hackers, and inadvertent errors.

e-mail (electronic mail): A form of communication that uses the Internet to send messages to other users; it requires an e-mail account and e-mail software.

e-mail software: A software application that allows users to send e-mail messages.

ergonomics: The science of fitting an activity or work space to a person's needs to ensure his or her comfort and productivity.

Ethernet: A local area network architecture that supports data transfer rates of 10 megabits per second (Mbps).

external storage: A method for storing computer data in a medium that can be removed from the computer itself (e.g., flash drives and CD-RW drives).

faceted browsing: The ability, in a library catalog, to limit a search by clicking on various facets or aspects of items included in the search results (item type, location, subject headings, etc.).

FAQ: A document containing answers to frequently asked questions; very common on the Internet as help guides to using a site or resource or as a source of detailed information on a topic.

federated search: A type of application that can be installed on a computer with Internet access or a network server that allows a user to search a variety of information sources at the same time; for instance, a library may wish to offer combined searches of their online catalog and their periodical databases from a single search blank.

feeds: The delivery of postings from a blog using RSS.

fiber-optic: A type of cable used in computer networks; tends to be more expensive than other cabling options but provides clear and quick transmission of data between workstations and servers; used extensively in telephone networks.

field: A section of a record in a database that holds a specific piece of information; for instance, in a MARC record for a book, there will be a field for the author's name.

56 Kbps modem: The top transmission speed for modems: 56 kilobits per second (Kbps).

file: A container of computer information that can be read or displayed by software applications (e.g., a word-processing file, an HTML file, or a file that makes up part of an application).

file server: *See* NETWORK SERVER.

filtering software: An application that is designed to restrict Internet users from viewing material that might be considered offensive.

firewall: A combination of software measures that restricts who can access information on a web server or network server; protects the server from being used or ruined by individuals who should not have access.

flash drives (also known as USB flash drives, pen drives, thumb drives, or key drives): Extremely small hard drives that can be used to move files, software, and even whole operating systems from computer to computer.

floppy disk: A 3.5-inch disk that can be used to externally store computer data, and can be removed from the computer and stored elsewhere or used to transport data from place to place; has a capacity of 1.44 megabytes (MB).

floppy drive: A device that is used to store data on a floppy disk.

folksonomy: A collection of information that has been classified by individual users' choices of terminology rather than by following a set classification system.

full text: A term used to describe the provision of the entire text of a periodical article or other source; an item described as "full text" should contain everything that appeared in the print version or other original format.

gateways: Devices used in wide area networking situations to help translate between local area networks that use different communication protocols.

gigabyte (GB): One billion bytes; common measurement of hard drive and storage space.

Gopher sites: Internet sites that are accessed using Gopher protocol, an older method for arranging and displaying information online; now superseded by the World Wide Web.

graphical user interface (GUI): A computer interface that allows you to interact with applications, Internet sites, and other items using a computer mouse to select graphical icons on your computer monitor.

hackerspace: An area, perhaps located in a library, in which individuals can use technology tools to create digital or physical items.

hard drive: An internal storage device for a computer workstation. Has the capacity to hold many different software programs and files. Current hard drive sizes are typically measured in gigabytes.

hardware: The physical devices that make up or can be used with a computer workstation (e.g., CPU, monitor, keyboard, printer, and scanner).

high-speed Internet access: Using DSL or a cable modem to access the Internet; much faster than dial-up Internet access using a standard modem.

host computer: Another way to describe a network server, which holds and serves, or hosts, a database or application of some kind; for instance, in order to run a library system, the library will need a server to host the system so that users can access it.

hyperlink: The ability to construct a word or image on a webpage that a user can click on to be linked to another website or document.

hypertext document: A web document created using hypertext markup language.

hypertext markup language (HTML): A series of tagged commands that can be used to construct a web document; HTML controls the formatting and interactivity of webpages with other files on the web (e.g., audio, video, images).

icon: Small graphical images that are used in computer operating systems and on the web as links to applications or documents.

identity theft: The capture of personal information and identification numbers from online databases by malicious parties.

image tag: In HTML documents, an element which controls how an image is displayed.

information technology: Any items or methods for containing, transmitting, and storing information.

input device: Used to enter information into a computer (e.g., a keyboard or mouse).

instant messaging (IM): Software that allows two individuals to send messages and files back and forth to each other in real time via the Internet.

integrated online library system (IOLS): *See* LIBRARY SYSTEM.

interface: The place in which we interact with a computer operating system, a library database, or anything else created or accessed using a computer; the interface is what displays on the screen as we use an application and controls how we can influence the application through keyboard or mouse commands.

internal storage device: A device that stores computer data, located within the computer's central processing unit.

Internet: The "network of all networks"; a worldwide computer network, first used in 1969, that has revolutionized communications and information exchange.

Internet access: The means by which an individual connects to the Internet to use its services.

Internet protocol (IP): A system for uniquely naming Internet servers to make it easy for individuals to connect to other network servers located anywhere in the world; each server on the Internet has its own IP number or address (e.g., 209.34.122.4).

Internet service provider (ISP): A company that provides Internet access to individuals or organizations for a fee.

intranet: A network that has limited its access to the members of a particular company or organization.

IP address: *See* INTERNET PROTOCOL.

iPad: A tablet produced by Apple.

iPod: An MP3 player produced by Apple.

ISBN (International Standard Book Number): Uniquely assigned to each book as an identifier; often a searchable field in library systems and acquisitions systems.

ITN (intention to negotiate): A call for bidders to respond with bids for a needed product; similar to an RFP but often less restrictive in terms of bidding rules.

keyword: A term that can be used to search a database or Internet search engine.

keyword searching: Gives users the flexibility to search all the information in a bibliographic record or a full-text periodical article to retrieve items that hold the keyword.

kilobyte (KB): One thousand bytes; equivalent to a short note on a single sheet of paper.

LCD (liquid crystal display): A technology that enables the creation of thin (flat-panel) computer monitors and data projection.

LCD projector: Display equipment that allows a user to project text, graphics, video, or live demonstrations of electronic library resources onto a screen.

learning management systems: Web-based products that provide a framework for web-based distance learning or web-supplemented teaching; the software allows instructors to post course materials, provide grades, and interact with students.

library system: A product that computerizes a variety of library functions including the public catalog, circulation, cataloging, acquisitions, and serials.

Linux: An open-source computer operating system developed with networking in mind.

local area network (LAN): A network that extends over a relatively small geographical area; can involve anywhere from two to several dozen workstations connected to a network server.

log-in ID: The username and password required to allow an individual access to a network.

Lynx: A text-based browser commonly used by individuals with visual disabilities.

Mac OS: The operating system for Macintosh computers.

machine-readable cataloging (MARC) record: An electronic record that contains a number of fields of information about an item in an online catalog (e.g., books, videos, Internet resources).

Macintosh: A computer developed in the early 1980s by the Apple Corporation; the first computer to popularize a graphical user interface and the use of a computer mouse.

magnetic media: Storage devices created by using electrical impulses to inscribe information in a certain pattern on magnetic material; examples include hard drives, flash drives, floppy disks, Zip disks, magnetic tape, videocassettes, and audiocassettes.

magnetic tape: A form of magnetic media primarily used for the archival storage of computer data; looks a lot like an audiocassette.

mainframe: A powerful computer used in the past to host library systems and other applications; now superseded by smaller network servers.

makerspace: An area, perhaps located in a library, in which individuals can use technology tools to create digital or physical items.

management software: Applications that assist with the operation of libraries; examples include a variety of office software tools that provide word-processing, spreadsheet, and database capabilities.

MARC: *See* MACHINE-READABLE CATALOGING (MARC) RECORD.

mashup: Any combination of multiple sets of data that results in a new online service.

media items: Audiovisual items.

megabyte (MB): One million bytes; equivalent to 200 to 300 pages of text.

megahertz (MHz): Common measurement of the internal speed of a computer's processor.

microfiche: A medium used to store miniaturized images of pages of text or diagrams on a small sheet of photographic film; a standard microfiche sheet can hold between 60 and 98 pages.

microfilm: A medium used to store miniaturized images of pages of text or diagrams on a roll of photographic film; microfilm can accommodate between 1,000 and 1,500 pages per 100-foot roll of 32 mm film.

microformat: A term used to speak about microfiche and microfilm formats together.

mirror site: A website that serves as a backup to another website in case of a system failure on the primary site.

modem: A device that translates the data a computer is sending into a format, or protocol, that can be sent through standard telephone lines at speeds up to 56 kilobits per second (Kbps); allows anyone with a computer, a modem, and a telephone line to gain access to the resources on a network.

module: A software program that handles a specific function within a library system (e.g., a circulation module).

monitor: A device that provides visual display of computer applications; monitors may be flat-panel devices, which are narrower and use LCD technology, or cathode ray tubes (CRTs), which are bulkier.

motherboard: A piece of circuitry that serves as the foundation for the workings of a computer.

mouse: A computer input device that controls applications through the movement of an arrow in a graphical user interface.

.mp3: A digital format for audio files; online audio and audio e-books are usually stored in this format.

multiple-user access: The ability for more than one user to access an electronic library resource at one time.

multitasking: The ability of a computer operating system to have multiple applications running at the same time and to allow users to switch back and forth among them.

netbook: A class of smaller-sized laptops with a focus on Internet access and network applications.

network: A method for sharing applications or information between two or more workstations; very common in the library world for sharing information resources.

network cabling: The cables that are used to connect the components of a network; common cable types include unshielded twisted pair, coaxial, and fiber-optic.

network interface card: A card that plugs into the motherboard of a computer to communicate with other computers through a network.

network operating system: Software used to manage access and operations in a network.

network server: A computer that is configured to offer applications, files, or other resources to the workstations connected to a network.

OC-3: A leased telephone line that can transmit data at 155 megabits per second (Mbps). These lines form the backbone of the Internet, quickly transmitting e-mail messages, files, and requests to view webpages from an individual's computer to another computer or server.

on-screen keyboard: A keyboard interface that displays on the computer screen and can be used by clicking on its keys with a mouse to enter text; helpful for those individuals with physical disabilities constraining their abilities to type with a standard keyboard.

online catalog (OPAC): *See* ONLINE PUBLIC ACCESS CATALOG (OPAC).

online pathfinder: A web document which contains lists of electronic and print resources that are useful for research in a particular topic area; the electronic resources can be directly linked to from the pathfinder.

online public access catalog (OPAC): The computer version of the card catalog; allows an individual to search the holdings of a library through an electronic interface.

online searching: The ability to search electronic versions of periodical indexes and other reference resources through a dial-up connection or the Internet.

OPAC: *See* ONLINE PUBLIC ACCESS CATALOG (OPAC).

open-source software (OSS): Software that is created by a collaborative group of individuals and then has its source code distributed to other programmers for them to alter; open-source software is often free (at no cost) but it is always freely available to anyone who wishes to use or improve on it.

OpenURL: A protocol that makes connections between databases that index periodicals and collections of full-text sources; an OpenURL server helps patrons see that an article citation in Database A is available in full text in Journal Collection B.

operating system: The environment in which all other software operates in a computer (e.g., Microsoft Windows and Mac OS).

optical character recognition (OCR): A process of using software to scan typewritten or printed copies of text and turn them into word-processing documents that can be manipulated.

original cataloging: A process in which a skilled cataloger examines an item and enters author, title, and publication information, as well as meaningful subject headings, into a cataloging system to create a MARC record for display in the online catalog.

parallel: One method for connecting scanners and other devices to a computer workstation, in this case using a parallel port on the central processing unit.

patron-driven acquisitions (PDAs): The process of placing records for e-books into a library's OPAC that allows patrons to discover the e-books; once patrons have clicked on an e-book a certain number of times, the item is purchased.

periodical: A publication that appears on some regular basis (e.g., magazines, journals, and newspapers).

periodical database: An electronic version of a periodical index. Can contain article citations, abstracts, and full-text articles.

peripheral: A variety of computer hardware items that have specific functions or capabilities (e.g., printers and scanners).

personal computer (PC): A computer workstation that includes a central processing unit, a monitor, and a keyboard and mouse.

personal digital assistant (PDA): A handheld computing device that can be used to keep a calendar, contain an address book, take notes, and access files created by various types of software.

physical security: Security measures put in place for the purpose of keeping library technology materials from being removed from the library (e.g., cabling or bolting equipment to work area furniture and utilizing a library security system to tag media items).

pop-ups: Internet browser windows with advertisements that suddenly appear as a user loads a website; pop-ups can be simply annoying or they may contain hidden links to download spyware.

presentation software: Computer software that allows a presenter to organize a collection of information and media into a professional presentation.

presentation technology: Allows information to be shared with an audience in a visual manner using display equipment, media items, and presentation software.

print catalog: *See* CARD CATALOG.

printer: A computer peripheral that is used to produce paper copies of information displayed in a computer application.

processor: A device that powers the calculations a computer must make to run software and process information. Located inside the central processing unit attached to the motherboard.

program: *See* SOFTWARE.

protocol: A format for communicating data through a network or between different networks (e.g., Internet protocol).

proxy server: A device that stands between public workstations and the Internet; can be used to allow those workstations to seamlessly connect to subscription databases or to restrict the workstations to access only preselected Internet sites.

radio frequency identification (RFID): A method used by libraries to protect their physical collections by placing a small tag on each item; tag consists of a computer chip with an antenna attached, and security gates or self-checkout systems can then read the tag to complete their functions.

RAM: *See* RANDOM ACCESS MEMORY (RAM).

random access memory (RAM): Memory cards that plug into a computer motherboard to give software temporary space to use while it is running. Generally, the more RAM a computer has, the faster it can operate.

real-time communication: Communication that happens on a synchronous basis, as in an in-person conversation (i.e., one person speaks and is heard by another person at the same time, then the two switch roles; there is no gap or loss of time in their interchange as there can be in Internet communications).

recon: The process of converting catalog cards to MARC records for each item in a library's collection when it moves to an online catalog.

record: A segment of a computer database that represents all the information on, say, one book or one article; information within a record is broken down into individual fields, which are typically searchable in online catalogs or periodical databases.

remote access: The ability for users to connect to library resources (e.g., websites, online catalogs, and periodical databases) from locations other than within the library.

remote information services: A corporate term for remotely accessed information sources such as Internet-based resources and those reached through the process of online searching.

removable storage: Devices that allow for the storing of computer data on media that can be removed from the central processing unit (e.g., flash drives, DVD-Rs and DVD-ROMs).

request for proposal (RFP): A process in which vendors respond to a written set of criteria for a needed product or service with detailed proposals of how they will meet the criteria; typically used with technology purchases that involve large amounts of money.

RFID: *See* RADIO FREQUENCY IDENTIFICATION.

routers: Devices that help exchange information between separate networks that are combined in a wide area network (e.g., the Internet).

RSS (rich site summary): A way of sending new postings to blogs out to RSS feed reader software or to individual websites.

scanner: A computer peripheral device that copies physical items (e.g., periodical articles and photographs) into digital form; the process requires that the device be connected to a computer and that the computer has scanning software installed on it.

screencast: The process of offering short video tutorials to library users to teach or review database searching or information literacy skills.

screen-reading software: Software that will read aloud whatever text appears on a workstation screen when it is installed and run on a workstation; it extends the accessibility of any material one can display on a workstation screen to those with no or extremely low vision.

search directory: Internet search tools that allow for keyword searching or topical browsing of human-built collections of websites and documents.

search engine: Internet search tools that allow for keyword searches of huge, robot-built databases of websites and documents.

server: General term for a computer that makes files, applications, or websites available to users of a network or the World Wide Web. *See also* NETWORK SERVER and WEB SERVER.

slide: (1) An individual screen or segment of a presentation created using presentation software; (2) an audiovisual format which uses small pieces of photographic film that can be projected on a screen (decreasing in number as an item found in library collections).

smartphones: Cell phones with computer functionality built in, including e-mail, web browsing, and other capacities.

software: Programs or applications that makes computers do what we want them to do; examples include operating systems, word processors, and Internet browsers.

sound card: A device that enables a computer to play sounds through speakers or record them through a microphone; plugs into the motherboard of the computer inside the central processing unit.

source aggregator: A term describing electronic library resource vendors that provide access to a large number of different information sources (e.g., periodical databases and full-text reference sources).

spam: Unwanted e-mail, often sent by advertisers.

spreadsheet software: A computer application used to compile budget and other statistical information in spreadsheet form.

spyware: Software that can be loaded on a workstation to track an individual's path online and record personal information.

stand-alone system: A library system that uses only a single module or a combination of nonintegrated modules that do not share data (i.e., a system that has just a cataloging module or that has a circulation module that does not automatically update the OPAC module when a book is checked out).

stylus: A pen-like device that can transmit commands and other inputs into the screen of a tablet.

synchronous: Refers to technologies used for communication or instruction that work in real time (e.g., chat or videoconferencing); users of these items are able to hold conversations as if they were talking in person.

T-1: A leased telephone line that can transmit data at 1.544 megabits per second (Mbps); used by organizations that require high-speed connections to the Internet.

tablet: A mobile device that allows direct input on its screen using a finger or, in some cases, a stylus; accesses the Internet with either or both cell or Wi-Fi access.

tagging: The practice of adding user-supplied descriptive terms to blog posts and other resources to create user-specific access points to content; tagging can also provide the larger community with additional terms beyond those in the Library of Congress Subject Headings to help in searching for information.

tape drive: Device used to save computer files on magnetic tape cassettes for archival storage.

technical support: The help provided by vendors for their products; technical support may be available at no charge for those who have purchased a product or it may be fee based, and is usually available only by telephone.

technology: A practical or industrial art that involves both products and processes invented by people.

technology plan: An attempt by a library to take inventory of its current technology, survey the needs of its users and its staff, and make a plan to acquire technologies to meet these needs.

teletypewriter (TTY): A device that users who have difficulty hearing can use to type messages back and forth with library staff members to access library information.

terminal: A device resembling a computer monitor with a keyboard that was used to access applications placed on a mainframe computer.

text-based: Refers to an application (e.g., database or library system) that does not make use of a graphical user interface but rather relies on text commands that are typed in.

touchpad: A computer input device that fulfills the functions of a mouse by having the user touch a flat pad to move the arrow on the screen.

trackball controller: A computer input device that fulfills the functions of a mouse by having the user move a ball with his or her palm to move the arrow on the screen.

troubleshooting: The act of investigating and solving technical problems with computer equipment, software applications, and other devices.

turnkey: A product (e.g., a local area network or a library system) provided by a vendor that includes all the necessary components so that all a library needs to do to start using it is to "turn the key" (i.e., press the power button); in this situation the product is also typically assembled on site by the vendor.

ubiquitous computing: The concept of computing and network resources being close at hand for individuals at all times; often this state is brought about by the use of mobile devices.

uniform resource locator (URL): The address of a website (or other Internet resource) that for the web take the form "http://" followed by the domain name and specific location of the site's files.

universal design: Making products and services usable by people with a wide range of skills and abilities.

UNIX: A computer operating system initially used only on mainframes that is widely used for large-scale networking purposes and on the Internet; tends to appear only on network servers and not on individual workstations.

unshielded twisted pair (UTP): A type of cable used in computer networks; used extensively for data transmission in libraries and educational institutions.

USB (Universal Serial Bus): A method for connecting peripheral computer devices to a central processing unit; now widely used because it provides high-speed communications between devices and the CPU and because it is easy to add many devices to the same USB port on the CPU.

Usenet: An asynchronous method of communications on the Internet that consists of posting questions, announcements, or replies to messages in a topical newsgroup; thousands of newsgroups are accessible using a web browser or a separate newsreader application.

vendor: A producer or seller of a product.

video card: A device that enables a computer to display images on its monitor that are generated by applications; plugs into the motherboard of the computer as part of the central processing unit.

videocassette: Also called videotape, an audiovisual or media format for recording video and sound for playback, consisting of a reeled, linear tape in a rectangular plastic case; from the late 1980s until very recently it was the most popular means for sharing and viewing video and is still widely available in libraries.

videodisc: An audiovisual or media format for recording video and sound for playback, consisting of a plastic or metal disc that can contain several hours of high-quality audio or video; laser discs, the original videodiscs, waned as a technology as the popularity of videocassettes and DVDs increased; by nature, DVDs and Blu-ray discs are also videodiscs.

virus: Computer applications designed to cause a destructive or harmful result, usually hidden in or attached to another program; once downloaded and run on an individual's computer, it can cause applications to malfunction and lock up; in extreme cases they can reformat hard drives or corrupt important system or data files.

voice-over Internet protocol (VOIP): The ability to transmit speech and video communications from computer to computer using Internet communications.

web server: A network server that hosts a website.

webinar: Informational or training presentation that is conducted entirely online, often through virtual classroom software.

webmail: This application allows accessing of e-mail online using a web browser rather than through locally applied software.

wide area network (WAN): A network that connects multiple local area networks (e.g., a network at a branch library connected with a network at the main library).

wiki: A website that can be edited and updated by anyone; often used for group editing of documents.

Windows: The computer operating system used for most PC workstations; a Microsoft product.

wireless network: A network in which radio signal and infrared transmission technologies allow computers to communicate with other workstations and network servers; makes use of devices called wireless access points to spread the wireless network within a building or throughout a broader area.

word-processing software: Application that is used for preparing memos, handouts, and other documents.

workstation: *See* PERSONAL COMPUTER (PC).

INDEX

You may also be interested in

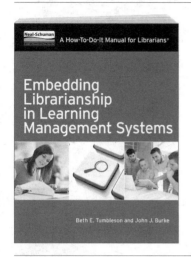